English Costume
from the Seventeenth through the Nineteenth Centuries

Iris Brooke

and

James Laver

DOVER PUBLICATIONS, INC.
Mineola, New York

Bibliographical Note

This Dover edition, first published in 2000, is an unabridged republication of the following sections from *English Costume from the Fourteenth through the Nineteenth Century,* "English Costume of the Seventeenth Century," "English Costume of the Eighteenth Century," and "English Costume of the Nineteenth Century," originally published in 1937 by The Macmillan Company, New York. Aside from this new arrangement of material, the only other alteration consists in retaining the color plates in black and white in their original position in the books, as well as including them all in a separate full-color insert with page number references to the text they illustrate.

Library of Congress Cataloging-in-Publication Data

Brooke, Iris.
    [English costume from the fourteenth through the nineteenth century]
    English costume from the seventeenth through the nineteenth centuries / Iris Brooke and James Laver.
       p. cm.
    Contains three sections of English costume from the fourteenth through the nineteenth century, originally published: New York : Macmillan Co., 1937.
    ISBN 0-486-41239-3 (pbk.)
     1. Costume—Great Britain—History. I. Laver, James, 1899– II. Title.

GT733 .B7 2000
391'.00942—dc21

                             00-031460

Manufactured in the United States of America
Dover Publications, Inc., 31 East 2nd Street, Mineola, N.Y. 11501

CONTENTS

English Costume
*from the Seventeenth through
the Nineteenth Centuries*

PART I

English Costume

of the

Seventeenth Century

FOREWORD

ALTHOUGH the aim and scope of the books in this series are self-evident to most readers, it seems desirable to touch on two points in this connection. In the first place, they are not intended for, nor would they interest, those who have made a life-study of historic costume and who are primarily concerned with the intricacies of the subject. My purpose is to provide a useful guide and not a serious text-book, to give elementary descriptions of costume for those who have neither time nor inclination to pore over countless prints, paintings, and actual examples, yet who wish to obtain a comprehensive idea of the dress of the period. The condensation of any aspect of a whole century into less than one hundred pages necessitates so high a degree of selection that many of its omissions and inclusions equally are open to debate. Nevertheless, to those with slight knowledge of the subject, wishing to select costumes from a certain decade in history, a book of this size is infinitely more useful than a tome fifty times its weight and extent, which would certainly give more detail but probably fewer actual examples of the complete costume desired.

Secondly, it is clear that detail cannot be dealt with beyond a certain measure of accuracy in full-length drawings of three or four inches high when the figure from which the costume is taken is usually life-size and sometimes larger. A minute study of such details as collars, belts, shoes, gloves, and dozens of other equally interesting items can be made satisfactorily only in the excellent collections of the articles themselves, such as are found, for example, in several of the museums in and around London.

The Stuart period is perhaps the most romantic in English

history, a period in which men duelled and danced, fought hard and loved hard, with equal grace and accomplishment, in satins and lace.   There was brutality enough and bitter feeling in the seventeenth century, war and suffering in abundance ; yet contemporary portraiture has preserved a remarkable appearance of unruffled exquisiteness.   These ghosts in wigs and ribbons, satins and silks, seem to live on more vividly than the historic facts with which they are surrounded—the Civil Wars of Cavalier and Roundhead, the Great Plague, the Fire of London, Monmouth's Rebellion, and the infamies of Judge Jeffreys.   Memorable as these events were, those who took part in them, unrivalled in history in their apparently haughty indifference to plagues, fires, wars, and massacres, have left a more enduring impression, an impression of gay bravado reflected in and emphasized by their extravagance in clothes.

                                                         I. B.

1660

1600—1610

SO little change is remarkable during the first ten years of the seventeenth century, that it will be unnecessary to dwell upon each portion of the fashionable garments in detail. The century opens with the flamboyant and ungainly clothing of Elizabeth's Court. Stiff, bombasted, and doll-like, these figures in ruffles, farthingales, exaggerated breeches, and quilted garments leave a lasting picture on one's mind.

Anne of Denmark, the new Queen, has long been famed for her complete lack of taste in clothes, and in her hands rested the reformation, or otherwise, of the existing fashions. Unfortunately, her fancy led her to encourage and exaggerate the already hideous and deforming costumes then prevalent at Court. History informs us that on the death of Elizabeth, her ladies proceeded to Berwick, to greet James I's queen, laden with the jewels and gowns of their late-lamented queen. If we are to believe the reputed size of the virgin Queen's wardrobe, it is not inconceivable that Anne should have converted a few hundred, at least, of these costly and regal gowns to her own use. If this were the case, it might possibly explain the seeming lack of progress in fashion during the ensuing fifteen years !

The farthingale—ugliest of all modes—continued in fashion and increased in size, in spite of the King's bad-tempered endeavour to exterminate it, until the death of Anne in 1619. It appears that at a grand masque at Court, several of the ladies became wedged in the passage, and so completely blocked the entrance, that half or more of the guests never managed to get into the hall or attend the masque. After this tiresome experience, James issued a proclamation forbidding the farthingale to be worn at Court ("This impertinent garment takes up all the room at Court") either by ladies or gentlemen—for the gallants not to be outdone by the fairer sex padded their breeches to a corresponding extent. No notice, however, was taken of this order, for the simple reason that the Queen flatly refused to abandon her favourite form of dress.

1600—1610 *(continued)*

Such fabulous sums were expended abroad on materials—silks, satins, velvets, etc., that one or two spirited endeavours were made to promote interest in the manufacture of materials at home. Mulberry farms were started in several parts of the country and silk-worms imported. Silk-growing survived for nearly a hundred years, and was only abandoned when the futility of protecting the mulberry trees in the chilly winter months was realized.

In the year 1599, William Lee, Master of Arts, at St. John's College, Cambridge, devised an " engine " or steel loom for knitting or weaving silk stockings, waistcoats, etc. From that date there were few ladies or gentlemen who denied themselves the luxury, comfort, and extravagance of silk stockings, even at £2 to £5 per pair.

The large sums paid for clothes seem out of all proportion to the salaries and incomes of the time. A plush cloak might cost £50; plush being sold at the ghastly price of £3. 10s. per yard (and exceedingly narrow it was, too); and of course, no garment was considered fit for a gentleman unless embroidered or guarded with lace or velvet. The importance of appearance may be seen in Ben Jonson's *Magnetic Lady*: " . . . He has stained my new white satin doublet and bespattered my spic and span silk stockings on the day they were drawn on, and here's a spot in my hose too "—this after a vulgar brawl.

Trimmings played just as important a part as they had during the sixteenth century; lace, ribbons, embroidery, artificial flowers, enamel, and jewels of all kinds, even coloured and gilded leather-work, were still placed indiscriminately on every garment—male or female. The Queen had a murrey-coloured satin gown ornamented with gilded cut leather sent her as a gift from the Queen of Spain. Breast-plates and collars of enamel and silver, or other fine metals, swords with embroidered and jewelled scabbards and sheaths, were frequently worn by men as part of their civil dress. Embroidered gloves, handsomely trimmed with fringe and tassels, were as necessary to the would-be élite as the embroidered and rosetted shoes.

1600—1610 *(continued)*

Long, loose gowns reaching to the ground, and trimmed with " shagg "—a long fur-like plush—or real fur, or even velvet, were worn by elderly gentlemen, or within the comparative privacy of one's own family circle. These gowns had the loose split sleeve, hanging from the shoulder, which formed the chief place of ornamentation. The breeches with canions, worn by the gentleman on the top right hand of the page facing, are composed entirely of heavy braid about an inch and a half to two inches wide—interlaced and sewn so as to leave a space through which a contrasting lining may be seen. With this form of nethergarment the stockings are tied just below the knees, and often hanging over the garter like the tops of boots. Overstockings, with leather soles and embroidered tops ; separate stocking-tops and boot-hose, were all worn at this period, and boots with coloured linings made of soft fancy leather were sometimes worn. It was not until the 'twenties, however, that the fashion was carried to an extreme. The large skirt-like breeches tended to elongate, giving them a squarish line at the knee, instead of the barrel shape of the earlier type ; to bring the latter more up to date, tassels and ribbons were frequently attached at the knee.

A kind of slipper, similar to a mule, with a heel about an inch or more in height, was worn to a considerable extent within doors. Doublets and bodices of embroidered linen were worn by both sexes, and often caps or bonnets of similar design, and edged with lace, were made to match. There is an example of a lady wearing one of the caps at the bottom of the opposite page ; and on the following page may be seen a gentleman in his indoor cap.

1600—1610 (*continued*)

Many and varied were the types of collar worn during this period—from the large Elizabethan ruffle to the flat lace collar worn by the little girl at the bottom of the second page of illustrations to this decade. A sufficiently comprehensive selection may be seen on these four pages.

In the year 1604 " James I by letter patents did incorporate the felt-makers of London, by the name of Hatter & Warders or Mistery of Feltmakers of London granting them divers privileges and liberties." Another endeavour to support home industries and thereby cut out the importation of Spanish and French beavers and felts ! Men's hats were overwhelmingly large and covered in feathers and jewels— and correspondingly expensive ! In Ben Jonson's *The Devil is an Ass*, the prize for a wager takes the form of " A new Four pound beaver hat, set with enamel studs." Any coloured hat was fashionable, although greys and blacks seemed most popular.

The hair-dressing or head-tiring of the ladies shows little or no difference from that of ten or even twenty-five years earlier. Quantities of jewellery was still worn in the hair, and saffron hair-dye remained a favourite tint. The black velvet hat with plumes of feathers still perched at an absurd angle on the back of the head, and any odd jewel or trinket that had not found a resting-place in my lady's periwig might be placed with impunity upon her hat !

1610—1620

ON the opposite page may be seen two excellent examples of the costumes of this period—the lady's taken from one of Anne's numerous portraits, and the other from a portrait of Henry, Prince of Wales. The extraordinary stiffness and impracticability of these clothes may be easily seen from these figures. It will be noticed that the bombasted breeches of the boy are split at the knee showing the lining—a fashion that became extremely prevalent during the 'twenties and 'thirties. The lined boots and boot-hose are also exceedingly advanced—as more of them are to be seen at a later date. The blue collar is an interesting point worthy of note, as, previously, collars had mostly been made of lawn, holland, or some white or natural-coloured material. The passion for decorating garments with gold braid or metal ribbon may be observed. Plain, indeed, was the doublet of this period if it were not ornamented with several yards of lace, embroidery, leather, bead-work, or braid. This suit was, in all probability, made of plush, of somewhat similar texture to the panne velvet of to-day.

This farthingale, similar to those worn by Elizabeth, was probably made according to the fashionable lady's requirements. " High at the back and low in the front, the sides wide, that I may rest my arms upon it." The collar was wired to keep it at the necessary angle to make a charming background to a well-painted picture !

Many hours' patient work were expended on my lady's toilet, many layers of clothes had to be fitted and fixed, and cosmetics had not yet arrived at any degree of perfection. The Spanish " papers " for rouge and powder did not arrive in England until many years later. A bag of chalk served the purpose of our modern powder-box !

1610—1620 (*continued*)

The last figure on this page has been specially inserted to show the arrangement of the skirt. To obtain the required outline, giant sausage-shaped horse-shoes of hair or rags were tied over the petticoat below the waist—the gown then being allowed to fall over this unwholesome piece of absurdity. This would account for the gown always being split up the front when the farthingale was worn, to facilitate the tying and arranging of the padding necessary to obtain the fashionable silhouette.

Ladies' hunting-suits or riding-habits of the day were not designed with the idea of giving any comfort to their wearers ; it was not even unusual to ride in a farthingale. If we are to take the portraits of the queen as typical of a fashionable lady's habit, we may perceive her dressed in a low revealing doublet, with stiff wired collar encircling the back of her head and neck, and making any neck movement difficult if not impossible. Full-padded sleeves split in the demands of fashion to expose the smock ; her skirts, if not actually concealing the farthingale—full-padded and trailing. An absurd hat of grey beaver, with a ridiculously high crown ornamented with feathers and enamel studs, perched unsafely on the front of her piled up hair.

The costume of the masked lady on the opposite page is also taken from a contemporary print of a group of ladies riding—although here the farthingale is small. It is difficult to imagine that a riding-suit of this sort could ever have been coped with, or worn with any degree of comfort. It will be noticed here that the lady is wearing a band under the chin—a device which appears to have accompanied the mask in various forms throughout the century. This particular mask was known as a Loo or half-mask.

Cuffs increased considerably during the decade, sometimes even being made in layers of three or four, and reaching above the elbow.

1610—1620 (*continued*)

An interesting variation of the immense breeches of the period may be observed at the top of the opposite page; these were cut on the lines of the open-breeches introduced some ten or fifteen years earlier, the gathering round the waist and the tightening of the hem giving a curious barrel effect. The doublet, too, is interesting in this example, as it shows a definite tendency to pad at the chest instead of having, as previously, all the padding near the belt. This latter fashion having survived in a much moderated form ever since the introduction of the Peas-cod doublet of the previous century.

After the death of Anne of Denmark, the ladies, having no leader to spur them on to further exaggerations and extravagances and no Court to dazzle with their magnificence, assumed a more subdued version of the previous fashions, and no longer vied with each other to wear the largest and most cumbersome petticoats, or the tallest head of hair most filled with jewels. And although one cannot, with any stretch of imagination, say that simplicity was the vogue, yet, after the extraordinarily bizarre and ostentatious fashions of the last quarter of a century, these ladies must have appeared amazingly subdued to one brought up in the wealthiest period of English History, and accustomed to the overdressed and over-bejewelled ladies and gentlemen at the Court of Good Queen Bess and the flamboyant Anne of Denmark.

From now onwards and until well into the eighteenth century the fairer sex held no light to the gallants in the matter of clothes. Every man had a thousand opportunities of adding a ribbon, a jewel, a fringe, a piece of lace, braid, rosette or curl; of showing an embroidered stocking, stocking-tips, costly boots, garters, and so on; whilst the woman must content herself with lace collars and cuffs, and perhaps a bunch of ribbons here or there.

1610—1620 (*continued*)

Beards and moustaches continued in favour until the 'eighties, and an amusing example of a beard, looking suspiciously artificial may be seen in the middle of the opposite page. The curly type of beard running round the chin to the jaw bones was most prevalent. This might be worn as in the picture of the man at the top of the page, or clipped to a point like that of the man at the bottom of the previous page. Men's hats had by now reached the height of their decoration—and price! Enamel studs and jewels of every kind found their place in the expensive hat-bands of the élite; and large metal or gold clasps, with coloured stones, were used to fix the feather decoration securely to the hat itself. So valuable were these hats that they were the first item to be removed by a highway thief or footpad. Men were lured within doors and their hats snatched before they had any idea who their assailant might be.

Gigantic pear-shaped pearls and stars, arrows, crescents, etc., were made in enamel and set with stones to wear in the hair. Pearls were so much worn at this time that even the edge of a collar might be closely set with these precious stones. The charming little lace-caps, already described, were not worn in England later than about 1618 or 1620. Caps were discarded for half a century or more in favour of a more elegant and informal type of hair-dressing. One notices that wherever the cap was worn in previous times the hair seemed to suffer in consequence. Few curls were allowed to escape from their hiding-place beneath layers of lace. Possibly the caps in history were invented for the busy woman who had no time for decorative hair-dressing, and just bundled up her hair beneath a cap, jammed on to hide any deficiencies.

1620—1630

THE first period of this decade was singularly lacking in advancement—or indeed any style at all. When the Queen died, James, devoid of feminine influence, had the Court cleared of women, and abandoned himself to drink and vice. The royal children had already been placed in the charge of various noblewomen about the country. The Court became a scene of carousing and debauchery, and fashions in England practically remained at a standstill. A few new modes filtered across the Channel, but until the vivacious and witty young Henrietta Maria arrived, bringing with her a Parisienne trousseau, the country had no one to lead them in fashions.

From the arrival on these shores in June 1625 of the daughter of France, a revolution in ladies' dress commenced. Gone were the farthingales, ruffles, and long stomachers. High short-waisted bodices with Medici collars, low revealing corsages, and soft silk petticoats reaching to the ground replaced the stiff brocaded, cheese-like short petticoats.

I have selected the garments on the opposite page—not because they are significant of 1620—but because they show a definite link between the new fashion and the old. The exact date of the woman's dress is probably about 1628, and the man's 1624. With the latter may be seen a shortening of the doublet together with an elongation of the "skirts" or "tassets"—the ruffle in its last form—breeches changing from the short "trunks" into knee-breeches with an ornamented hem.

The lady's dress still holds something of the stiffness of Elizabethan times—the long stomacher is there, but the new high waist-line is emphasized by a ribbon tied under the arm-pits. The petticoat is short—while the gown assumes the new length touching the ground. The hair is dressed in a definitely transitional stage; it is still crimped and drawn back from the forehead, but a tiny fringe is visible, and a few small curls are allowed to hang over the ears, which for several years had been displayed. Later it will be noticed the fringe developed into a row of neat curls, and the side-curls became more and more exaggerated until the 'nineties.

1 6 2 0—1 6 3 0 (continued)

Few of the drawings on these four pages represent clothes worn earlier than 1625, as the advancement between 1618 and 1625 was so slight. With Charles I comes a difference. Before the stereotyped dress associated with this unhappy king became prevalent, for a few years there was a slightly experimental stage. Doublets were many and varied in design; some in the French style with the square-cut skirts, so beautifully illustrated by Abraham Bosse, were introduced in about 1628. The leather jerkin, sleeveless and reaching half-way down the thigh, was worn by civilians as well as by the Militia of that time. These continued in favour until well into the 'sixties; sometimes they were devoid of decoration—sometimes fringed and ornamented at the hem and arm-holes.

Leg-wear by about 1627 or 1629 had taken the form of loose knee-breeches, tied or sewn down the side to within five or six inches of the knee, and from there to the garter gaping open to show the fine lining. An example of this may be seen on the top right-hand figure on the opposite page. Some of the breeches had fringe or lace at the knee, and often stockings with decorated stocking-tops were tied just below the knee, giving the same effect as an edge. These stocking-tops were worn over the ordinary stockings; the habit of wearing two or more pairs seems prevalent from about 1625 until the end of the century.

Boots and boot-hose increased in size and decoration—the bucket-topped boot becoming a necessary part of every would-be gallant's attire. Large flaps of a butterfly shape were worn over the instep of these monstrosities. Several contemporary satirists depict the fop straddling along in a ludicrous and ungainly walk impeded and finally tripped up by his enormous boots. Bows of ribbon and gigantic rosettes decorated the square, elongated toes of their shoes.

The rather attractive fashion of tucking up the petticoats was started towards the end of this decade—probably when the longer gowns were introduced and the ladies had some difficulty in negotiating the notoriously filthy streets without ruining their fine garments. At first the gowns were held up by hand, but later they were pinned or tied in a variety of fashions. The high-waisted, tabbed bodice diminished in length as it increased in width—the increased size of the sleeves and wide, pointed collars adding several inches to the shoulders of their wearers.

1620—1630 (*continued*)

Ladies' sleeves were often composed of three separate materials. First the sleeve of the "smock," or shift, of some fine holland or silk, and over this a multitude of ribbons reaching from shoulder to wrist tied below the elbow and revealing the lining as the ribbons fell from the arm. Over this ribbon was the short elbow-length sleeve belonging to the bodice or gown. This was cut to the epaulet on the shoulder in front and tied at the elbow, frequently reaching only across the back of the arm—as shown in the example at the top of the opposite page. The full sleeve was still worn a great deal, and there are a few examples before the 'thirties of a three-quarter length sleeve —as will be seen at the bottom of the opposite page. This style, however, did not become the rage until five or six years later.

On the previous page will be seen a girl in the peasant costume of the day. As this type of dress was worn for several years by the working-class, it will be unnecessary to frequently repeat it.

The period of lace had begun—lace cuffs, lace collars, lace at the wrist and knees, lace on gloves and stockings, lace even on hats, and every fine garment was "laced." Where previously a tiny edge of lace had been, a deep border took its place. Right through the century and well into the eighteenth the most beautiful and exquisite lace played an important part in the decoration of clothes.

1 6 2 0 — 1 6 3 0 (*continued*)

Veils became fashionable towards the end of the 'twenties. They were worn without a hat and consisted of a square piece of net laid over the head and reaching about as far as the mouth, the border often of lace.   One of these is illustrated in the next group of heads (1630–1640).   Hairdressing became more and more informal—the effect of nonchalance in the arrangement of the curls was belied by the neatness of the back-view.   At first the hair was puffed at the sides, giving an effect of short hair from the front; later, the front curls were cut shorter, or added, in cases where nature had not been sufficiently generous for the demands of fashion. From this time onwards until the introduction of the pinner or commode in the late 'seventies, fashionable ladies wore no hats or head-dresses, with the exception of hoods, that were not equally suitable for men.   The large beavers and felts, and even velvet caps, were exact replicas of their husband's or brother's.

Feathers decorated practically every hat.   Long curling plumes of ostrich feathers stuck out from the hat-bands and drooped over the shoulders of the gallants, mingling with their locks, now worn long.   The shoulder-length curls were now allowed to grow several inches over the collar. Some of the older men still adhered to the mode of short hair, but men of all ages wore the fashionable Van Dyck beard and moustaches, the brighter sparks curling their moustaches to ridiculous extremes, and clipping their beards to a sharp point.

The ruffle, having quite disappeared by 1627, was supplanted by the now famous Van Dyck collar.   Made of the most exquisite lace, they reached from the throat to points over the shoulders.   The stiffened pleated Medici collar remained in favour until the 'fifties.

1630—1640

THE cut of the doublet on the opposite page is typical of the 'thirties. Often the front was slashed in two or three places to show the shirt. The breeches were tied to the doublet at this time, with points threaded through the eyelet holes round the waist above the tabs or tassets. The epaulet was still worn on the shoulders of every doublet. Sleeves varied only slightly, all being formed of ribbons reaching from shoulder to wrist. Sometimes they were joined just below the elbow, and the forearm in this case was tightly fitting, but usually they hung loosely, showing large puffs of silk shirt. Cuffs were all made of lace or embroidered linen. The collar was edged with fine lace; in this instance it is supported round the face, although this type of collar was rarely seen after 1630, the popularity of the Van Dyck collar sweeping other modes before it.

Children of either sex wore these charming little caps until they were four or five years old, little girls wearing them until they were eight or ten years of age. The pinafore or apron, decorated with fine lace, was worn by little girls throughout the entire century.

The embroidered bodice of the lady is very similar in design to that of her spouse—the same type of sleeve being equally fashionable for either sex. The ladies' costumes at this period were very subdued in contrast to those worn ten or twenty years earlier. Plain materials were more to be seen than patterned, and a lace collar and cuffs were often the only form of adornment.

The Queen was not extravagant in clothes, the duties of a mother claiming all her attention. In one of her letters she writes to France asking for a new petticoat-bodice, as she has nothing but a velvet one which she had two years previously, and that is worn and too short and tight to be fashionable. This modest request stands out in history after the ridiculous quantities of garments the two previous queens had indulged in. Of all the accusations hurled at this unhappy Queen, nothing could be said about her personal extravagance. The only other mention of wearing apparel in Henrietta Maria's letters seems to have been a request for one dozen pairs of sweet chamois gloves and one of doeskin.

1630—1640 (*continued*)

By 1630 all signs of padding and stuffing in the breeches had disappeared. They now hung loosely, fitting the leg to the knee, where they were usually tied with a lengthy and wide garter wound several times round the leg, and then tied in a large bow or arranged as a rosette. Boots continued in size and decorativeness and were rarely worn without the boot-hose, or stocking-tops, hanging over the turned-down top. The figure of the small boy at the top of the page is taken from a portrait of William of Orange, and it is interesting to note that as early as '39, the short coat was worn in the Netherlands, when it did not become prevalent in England until the 'forties. This example has the sleeves and slashing of the 'thirties, also the collar.

Ladies' hair was worn longer than previously, " heartbreakers," or long curls, being arranged to fall over the shoulders. Hair ornaments of pearls and ribbon were worn a great deal at either side of the " bun " at the back, and showing from the front. Little girls wore, what would to-day be called hair-ribbons, to tie their curls back from their forehead—as may be seen at the top of the opposite page.

The stomacher was nearly always cut in a U shape below the waist. The neck-line of the bodice no longer formed a V in front, a square being much more fashionable. This was usually very low cut, and often a tiny frill of lace protruded from the top of the bodice. Long strings of pearls were exceedingly fashionable, often being worn to emphasize the waist-line, and tied in a variety of fashions at the neck and waist.

Cuffs might fall softly from the three-quarter length sleeve or they might turn back, their " raggs " or points reaching to the elbow. Furs, stoles, or tippets were worn during the 'thirties; and the first umbrella appeared in England in this decade.

1630—1640 (*continued*)

So many are the brilliant drawings of Abraham Bosse, the son of a French tailor, and Wenceslaus Hollar during this period, that it is extremely difficult to make a selection of typical garments from the vast quantities available. The French and English styles differ a little, but as both must have been worn in England—Henrietta Maria never forgetting unfortunately that she was a Frenchwoman—both styles must be represented. The muff tied in the centre with ribbon, and the box-pleated petticoat are both amusing and unexpected. The mock-sleeves on the little child's gown are unusual at so advanced a period of the seventeenth century.

Capes, from the 'thirties onwards, were an indispensable part of every man's attire, and they were worn *under* the collar of the doublet. Hats became larger and with higher crowns as the 'forties approached. The French method of men's hairdressing consisted of a fuzzy bush of untidy curls around the face and head with several long curls hanging down the back; whilst in England the more favourite method of dressing the hair was in a long curly "bob," resting on the collar in a layer of well-ordered ringlets. Moustaches and beards continued in favour, and varied but slightly from the style of ten years earlier.

The little maid-servant at the bottom of the page has her hair tucked away in a cap—one of the few examples of a cap of any sort worn during this period. She is fixing the extra collar on her mistress's dress. These collars were worn over the square-shaped ones, and in many contemporary portraits it is possible to see right through the outer collar of fine material to the neckline of the dress itself, which was always square in front.

Furs, gloves, masks, hoods, and veils were all important etceteras of the ladies' possessions. An interesting item which was worn from about 1630 to the end of the century was the little shoulder-cape, worn whilst the hair was being arranged and with practically any form of deshabille.

1630—1640 *(continued)*

The first example here is the back view of the French fashion in men's hairdressing—a bow of ribbon is here attached to the longest lock. This craze for odd bows of ribbon in the hair—ornamental perhaps, but entirely useless—remained fashionable for about thirty years, in fact until the periwig took the place of natural hair.

Black net veils were worn to protect the ladies' complexions from the harmful rays of the sun. Freckles and sunburn were considered harmful and disfiguring. To our minds this careful covering of the face, but exposure of the neck and head to the full blaze of the summer sunshine seems particularly stupid; no doubt, however, the lily-skinned beauties of the 1630's would regard our sun-tanned faces as distinctly unladylike and probably indecent.

During the winter months, still greater care was taken to prevent the skin from being roughened or exposed to the chilly winds. A hood completely encircling the face was worn, a mask covered the forehead and nose, and a chin-band was snugly arranged to conceal the jaw, so that the entire face was hidden except the mouth. Furs were worn extensively so that the ladies could snuggle under them, as we do to-day, in the teeth of an East Wind. It is questionable whether their complexions really benefited by all this tender care, but if their skins were soft and peach-like, it is, alas! impossible for us now to discover, or we might possibly be persuaded to follow in their footsteps.

The large flat-brimmed beaver or felt hat was first seen in about 1638. This style afterwards developed into the high-crowned hats of the 'forties, and the large Puritan hats worn by the Parliamentary party must have been designed from one similar to the example on the opposite page.

1640—1650

THE 'forties were turbulent and restless years; the Civil Wars breaking up the country into two distinct parties, each with their own dress, and each going to opposite extremes with their exaggerations.

The gown and suit on the opposite page show the somewhat moderated gloom of civil attire, though the man is definitely of Cavalier tendencies, judging by the bows of ribbon on his love-locks. These clothes also show the short-lived popularity of the sober dress associated with this period.

Mrs. Hutchinson, in the *Memoirs* of her husband, says : " When Puritanism grew into a faction the zealots distinguished themselves, both men and women, by several affections of habit, looks, and words, which had it been a real declension of vanity and embracing of sobriety in all those things had been most commendable in them ; but their quick forsaking of those things when they were where they would be showed that they either never took them up for conscience' sake or were corrupted by their prosperity to take up those vain things they durst not practice under persecution. Among other affected habits, few of the Puritans, whatsoever degree they were of, wore their hair long enough to cover their ears, and the ministers and many others cut it close round their heads, with so many little peaks as was ridiculous to behold—from this custom of wearing hair the name of roundhead became the scornful term given to the whole Parliament party." Colonel Hutchinson wore his hair long and curled—and, indeed, had a very fine head of hair, fanatical Puritan though he was. We may also suppose that he did not affect the ordinary Puritan garb, as his wife speaks of a handsome red velvet doublet of his.

1 6 4 0—1 6 5 0 (*continued*)

The Cavaliers took good care that they should not be mistaken for the opposing party, and exaggerated every fashion to the point of ridicule. The short coat, barely reaching to the waist, displayed quantities of fine shirt—and ribbons were attached to the hems of every garment. Breeches—which had assumed the proportions of a skirt by the 'fifties, were, for the most part, knee-length, and hung loose, the better to show off layers of ribbon or lace. The sides often had bows or rosettes attached—this form of ornamentation eventually resolving itself into a panel of lace or ribbon, or both, from waist to hem. The tighter form of knee-breeches was still worn, and embroidered stockings, tied up or pinned above the knee on to the breeches, were often seen, as in the figures on the top right hand of the opposite page.

Both these figures are wearing clothes more suitable to the Parliamentarians than the Royalists. Capes were extensively worn during this period, and it was also during the 'forties that the ladies' waist-line once more dropped to normal; the exaggerated sleeves became less inflated and the neck-line lower. A curious item about the Puritan collar is worthy of note : the collar seems to have been an entirely separate affair, pinned at the throat and dropping over the shoulders, the Λ-shaped space in front revealing a low-necked bodice with an expanse of uncovered chest. One of these collars is worn by Elizabeth Cromwell in a contemporary miniature, and, although she wears the traditional Puritan bonnet, her hair beneath is revealed in careful ringlets.

Long aprons of finest lawn with a tiny lace edge became a part of fashionable attire during this period; previously they had been worn only by children and domestics. A loose shoulder-cape was often worn by ladies to give additional warmth, and muffs and furs played an important part in every winter wardrobe.

1640—1650 (*continued*)

At the bottom of the opposite page will be seen a messenger boy or page in his trunk-hose. This form of nether garment was worn throughout the century by page-boys and as a Court-dress on a great many occasions.

The subdued tone and comparative simplicity of the ladies' attire at this time was probably due to the dangers a well-dressed woman was exposed to should any Parliamentarian set foot in her house. Any form of ostentation, for a few years at least, was viewed with definite disfavour.

The Cavalier light-heartedly stepped into the fray, taking an absurd delight in showing his bravery and royalty, though trammelled with feathers, lace, and love-locks. His absurd boots probably impeded him, but rather than discard one item of finery he preferred to flaunt his allegiance to the sovereign as long as the King drew breath.

In contrast a contemporary writer describes the Parliamentary party : " In high-crowned hats, collar bands, great loose coats, with long swords under them, and calves' leather boots."

The absurd fashions eventually triumphed over the more sedate fashions favoured by the Parliamentarians, and, as Mrs. Hutchinson mentions in her *Memoirs*, if any one had seen the " Roundheads " even a couple of years after their first heated demonstration of Purity—it would have been impossible to see the reason for their name.

1640—1650 (*continued*)

Ladies of Royalist inclination wore their hair in a long thick mass of curls, covering their shoulders and adorned with numerous bows of ribbon. As will be seen in the figure on the previous page, the back hair was still neatly arranged. The lady with the curls on the opposite page happens to be taken from a contemporary miniature of Cromwell's daughter, Mrs. Ireton, so that despite her Puritan tendencies her vanity was not sufficiently subdued for her to abandon and forsake her curls, in favour of the Puritan cap; neither do her scantily-draped shoulders indicate the modesty required of Ireton's wife. Altogether, after studying the period, these Parliamentarians seem to have been a set of fanatical humbugs—with the exception, of course, of the Puritan Fathers, who were so disgusted with the vanities and immorality in England. They set themselves a rigid and austere code of life, and abandoned the country so saturated with vice, for a new World where they could practise what they believed, untrammelled by the persecution and ridicule to which sobriety and modesty had previously exposed them.

In the year 1649 Cromwell passed an Act "For the relief of felt-makers and hat-band-makers against aliens and strangers." In spite of James I's efforts, apparently, to promote the hat industry in England, foreign competition was again getting the upper hand. It is curious that Cromwell should interest himself in anything so trivial during the year of the execution of the unhappy Charles.

It is recorded in Henrietta Maria's *Memoirs* that it was she herself who originally gave the name of "Roundhead" to the Cromwellian party. Seeing for the first time this curious fashion in a Parliamentary demonstration, and being struck by one of their number, she remarked: "La! What a handsome roundhead!"

1650—1660

ENGLAND during the Commonwealth gives one the impression of sobriety and modesty, yet curiously enough, if we are to believe the writers—or the artists—of that day, though the latter are more conspicuous by their absence than at any other period in history, England continued to light-heartedly proceed in her extravagances and fopperies.   Even without the evil example of the extravagant and reckless Court, and in spite of the crushing and bigoted influence of the Protector, the majority of the men still wore their hair long and curled, and had bows of ribbon tied to their love-locks.   Ladies still wore patches on their faces to attract attention to their dimples, or other attractive features, and, what is even more extraordinary and unexpected, we learn from an entry in *Evelyn's Diary* in the year 1654 : " . . . I now observed how the women began to paint themselves, formerly a most ignominious thing and only used by prostitutes."

In the entry above this surprising piece of news we learn that he did " Visit the Mulberry Gardens, now the only place of refreshment about towne for persons of the best quality to be exceedingly cheated at ; Cromwell and his partisans having shut up and seized on Spring Gardens, which till now had been the usual rendezvous of ladies and gallants at this season."   This hardly strengthens or confirms the idea of the domesticated and reformed ladies and gentlemen, virtuously renouncing the " pomps and vanities of this world," especially as John Evelyn was an excellent and worthy gentleman of a religious turn of mind.

On the opposite page will be seen the, to us laughable, habit of the dashing gallant.   His absurd jacket still retains something of the tasseted skirts in the form of two-inch flaps—these flaps disappeared entirely during the 'fifties. The turned-up hat was decorated equally on both sides : a frill of lace laid round the edge of the brim and a large bunch of coloured ribbons balancing the feathers on the other side.

1650—1660 (*continued*)

Several entries from the *Diary* of Samuel Pepys in the year 1659 give us an idea of the importance attached to clothes at this period—especially those worn by this amusing humbug himself.   Remembering that Pepys was the son of a tailor, and therefore as appropriately attired as the figures illustrated by Abraham Bosse, also the son of a tailor, twenty or thirty years previously, one must consider him as a definite authority on the subject.

On January 1, 1659, he writes : " This morning I rose, put on my suit with great skirts, having not lately worn any other clothes but them." (This is probably similar to the last suit on the opposite page.) However, the same suit was discarded the following month in favour of " My white suit with silver lace coat," and about the same time he wears a " Jackanapes coat with silver buttons " ; none of which sound at all Puritanical.   He presents his wife with £5, to buy herself a petticoat (after spending three or four times as much on himself), and receives an unpleasant shock when she returns to him and, apparently innocently, tells him that his father has persuaded her to buy a fine cloth at twenty-six shillings a yard, and please may she have some more money as it must have some fine lace upon it !   On the following Sunday he expresses his regret that the petticoat " makes no great show," being " light coloured and lace all over silver."   But he takes care that she treats this expensive garment with due care, and severely reprimands her when she leaves it untidily in the bedroom.   This historian tells us that shoes were exceedingly uncomfortable when new, and he frequently records the agony of wearing a new pair of shoes.   One entry describes their walk to church with his wife wearing new footwear : " My wife exceedingly troubled by a pair of new pattens and I vexed to go so slow."

1650—1660 (*continued*)

Riding-habits seem to have been exactly similar to men's suits. A lady's riding-habit described by Pepys several years later, was probably designed in a similar manner to the example opposite. He writes : " Walking in the galleries I find the Ladies of Honour dressed in their riding garbs, with coats and doublets with deep skirts, just for all the world like mine, and buttoned their doublets up the breast, with perriwig and with hats : so that, only for a long petti-coat dragging under their men's coats, nobody could take them for women in any point whatever ; which was an odd sight, and a sight did not please me." The effeminacy of his own clothing obviously did not strike him.

Men's heads, before the fashion for periwigs became general, were decorated and curled to ridiculous extremes. Each curl that fell over the gallant's shoulder must be adorned with a bow of ribbon—sometimes even the back curls were divided and tied. The crowns of hats were often eight or nine inches in height, and the brims received divers attentions in the complicated arrangements of ribbons, lace, feathers, and plumes.

1650—1660 (*continued*)

In contrast the ladies' heads must have seemed small; curls were not worn to any great excess, unless the wearer was blessed with natural curls, the hair being dressed with merely a slight wave and rarely reaching lower than the chin.   Fine jewels and pearls still adorned the head, but it was not until after the Restoration that the hair was extravagantly dressed.   The back-view of the hood on the opposite page shows how it was gathered to allow the kiss-curls at the nape of the neck to be clearly seen.

It is probable that as widows were so much in evidence during this decade that the heavy weeds worn previously became an unwarrantable expense and an indication of their political inclinations.   At all events, the charming little peaked black cap with the white lining became a fashionable and exceedingly attractive form of mourning.   The heavy veiling was probably rejected by the Royalists as being too sombre to express their extravagant views, and too similar to the dreary uniform adopted by the Puritan fanatics.

1660—1670

WITH the arrival of Charles II into England, and the reinstallation of a Court—fresh outbursts of wild gaiety and rejoicings led the country into a whirl of thoughtless extravagance and immorality.

John Evelyn writes of the King's coronation in 1661: "Clad in the fantastig habits of the time the magnificent traine or horseback, as much as embroidery, velvet, cloth of gold and silver, and jewels, could make them and their pransing horses, proceeded through the streets strewed with flowers, houses hung with rich tapestry, windoes and balconies full of ladies."

The same spirit of intoxication seems to have continued for several years, and with it the squandering of vast sums upon clothes and articles of adornment.

Curiously enough the men far surpassed the women in their overdressing—some of the ladies looking positively sombre in contrast to the feathered, laced, and beribboned gallants. Rather charming were the little black velvet coats edged with white fur of Dutch origin, as worn by the lady in the frontispiece page. Their simplicity strikes a quaint note in contrast to the ladies' flowered and laced garments. Lace played such an important part in the clothes of the day that no lady wished to be without at least one gown "laced all over."

Pepys has great difficulty with his wife in this particular. After forbidding her to go to the extravagance of buying one of these gowns—her new one arrives covered in lace, and her old one also appears with narrow lace "all over"— she seemingly surprised at this error! Pepys also notes on August 29, 1660: "This is the first day that ever I saw my wife with black patches since we were married." Patches had, however, been introduced towards the end of Charles I's reign.

Both long coats and "jackinapes," or short waist-length coats, were worn at this period. Some of the latter type of suit were carried to ridiculous absurdity—as in the example at the bottom of the opposite page. Ribbons of several different shades were worn on the same garment, or sometimes embroidered ribbons or multi-coloured ribbons.

The collars of the suits at this time continued to be high and stiffened—the cravat being worn over the coat and entirely separate.

1660—1670 (*continued*)

In the year 1665 Evelyn (according to himself) suggests a new mode of attire after the " Eastern Fashion," which the King light-heartedly adopts for a short time.   Unfortunately no examples of this type of dress remain, although both Pepys and Rugge mention it.   Evelyn's records on October 18 of this year : " To Court.   It being the 1st time his Majesty put himself solemnly into the Eastern Fashion of vest, changeing doublet, stiff collar, bands, and cloake, into a comely vest, after the Persian mode, with girdle or straps, and shoe-strings and garters into bouckles of which some were set with precious stones, resolving never to alter it, and to leave the French mode, which had hitherto obtained to our greate expense and reproch.   Upon which divers courtiers and gentlemen gave his Majesty gold by way of wager that he would not persist in resolution." And by the 30th of that month he had himself adopted these clothes : " To London to our office, and I had on the vest and surcoat or tunic as 'twas call'd, after his Majesty had brought the whole court to it.   It was a comely and manly habit, too good to hold, it being impossible for us in good earnest to leave the Monsieurs vanities long."   Pepys describes the "Eastern Fashion" : " Being a long cassocke close to the body, of black cloth, and pinked with white silk under it, and a coat over it and legs ruffled with black riband like a pigeon leg."

And Rugge : " Viz. a close coat of cloth pinkt with a white taffety under . . . This in length reached the calf of the leg, and upon that a surcoat cutt at the breast, which hung loose and shorter than the vest 6 inches.   The breaches of the Spanish cut, and buskins some of cloth some of leather, but of the same colour as the vest or garment."

Possibly this attire was similar to the long coats worn by young boys.   Boys frequently remained long-coated until they reached the age of twelve or thirteen.   I have not here illustrated this fashion ; it is sufficient to say that it closely resembles the coats still worn by the Blue Coat boys to-day.

The fashion in England of wearing the skirts tucked up, tied up, and pinned up, continued in favour throughout the century, and was an excellent excuse for ladies to wear two beautiful petticoats instead of one.

The waist-line continued to move downward.   Jewellery —especially pearls, were necessary accessories to any well-dressed woman.   Pepys buys his wife a necklace of pearls —three rows for £80, and another at an earlier date for £4, 10s., so that apparently any price might be paid for these baubles.

1660—1670 (*continued*)

Periwigs became more and more prevalent, in the year 1663, Pepys has his hair cut—buys a periwig for £4, and has his own hair made into another for 25s. Ladies wore them only in riding-dress, and then over their own hair. Frequently, however, artificial curls were worn attached to the sides of the head. Hats were still large and decorated with feathers, although as the 'seventies approach the tall hat becomes less fashionable, and the large-brimmed hat with a low crown increases in favour. This hat was the forerunner of the tricorn worn throughout the eighteenth century. By about 1670 some of the hats took on a definitely three-cornered aspect.

Feminine head-dressing was somewhat severe at this period, the hair being drawn back from the face and arranged in an oval "bun" at the back—the "bun" being tied each side with ribbons, or decorated with gems or artificial flowers. Curls were worn at the side of the face resting on the shoulders, and a short-curled fringe or sometimes a row of tiny curls adorned the forehead—these were termed "Cruches."

Hats were rarely worn by the fairer sex—the hood disarranging the hair less, and infinitely more camouflaging should the owner wish to go abroad masked to an illicit rendezvous. With cloak, hood, mask, and fan, little or no chance of recognition was possible.

It will be noticed from the accompanying illustrations that ladies' neckwear was either *décolleté* in the extreme or the exact reverse—one's collar was either to one's throat or else did not begin till after the shoulders were exposed; in either case lace or fine net must be the only material used.

Pepys mentions his "Best black cloth suit trimmed with scarlet ribbon, very neat, and my cloake lined with velvet— a new beaver, which altogether is very noble with my black silk knit canions"—canions in this case meaning the over-stockings worn loose and dropping down like a boot, and similar to the examples on the previous page. In 1668 he puts on "A New Stuff suit with a shoulder belt according to the new fashion and the bands of my vest tunique laced with silk lace of the same colour." These shoulder bands may also be observed in the drawings.

Black was an exceedingly fashionable colour; Pepys mentions several black suits of his, and a black silk dress of his wife's "laced all over with black lace point."

1670—1680

THE period of the short coat had definitely come to an end by about the year 1668. The long-skirted type of coat once installed, remained in favour for over a century. These coats were first worn with a belt or sash tied round the waist, and a long waistcoat of varying length reaching from shoulder to the middle of the thigh, or to the bottom of the coat was specially fashionable. Breeches were often made of black velvet, contrasting with a coloured coat, and these continued to be ornamented with ribbons, lace, and fringe for several years after the installation of the skirted coat. Ornamental sword belts, or shoulder belts as they were often termed, were worn a great deal as part of the necessary civil dress. The sleeve of the coat rarely reached below the elbow, and was turned back in an elaborate cuff—cut in a variety of complicated designs. Often the waistcoat had long sleeves, and these were sometimes turned back over the cuff of the coat-sleeve. Occasionally they were worn tight nearly to the wrist, from whence the luxurious lace-frills of the shirt bunched out in a cascade of lace and silk. Ribbons were still worn at shoulder, elbow, and knee, and beautiful embroideries adorned the split skirt at the back of the coat, down the facings and the pockets. The cravat was usually tied with a small bow of ribbon—this fashion later developed into the stiff formal arrangement of scarlet ribbons.

The periwig took on vast proportions during the 'seventies, and increased in size until about 1710—when it was supplanted by the white wig. Boots were not often worn except for riding—the fashionable form of footwear being that with a high tongue or flap reaching from four to six inches above the instep.

The gentleman on the opposite page has his " flaps " cut in an ornamental fashion, and falling down over the buckle ; these were usually lined with silk or a contrasting shade of leather. Heels were high and sometimes red. An excellent example of the type of breeches worn on the opposite page may be seen at the Victoria and Albert Museum.

1670—1680 *(continued)*

Ladies' fashions definitely changed during the 'seventies. Not only the hairdressing, but practically every item altered slightly. Trains were often worn at Court, and at other times the skirts were drawn back in a somewhat formal manner giving the effect of a bustle. The fashionable bodice was very tight and low-waisted, with a tiny sleeve either pinned up or turned back well above the elbow. High collars were not so prevalent as the low neckline dropping off the shoulders at the side and forming a **V** in front. Flowered taffety, moire, and flowered tabby were favourite materials—floral patterns being more in use from the 'seventies onwards than previously, and a patterned material was more usual than one decorated with lace and ribbons. All these silks were exquisitely embroidered by hand, and the designs were amazingly naturalistic in manner. So beautiful were these minute posies that it seems almost incredible to us in this age of hustle and bustle that any human being could find the time and have the inexhaustible patience to cover dozens of yards of silk with almost invisible stitches.

The smocks or under-garments at this period had immense bunched and gathered sleeves—infinitely fuller than those of the bodice and always decorated with a deep frill of lace or embroidery. Several hundred illustrations would be an inadequate reference to seventeenth-century ornamentation. Unfortunately there is no opportunity for even a few examples of small details of lace and embroidery ornamentation to be inserted in these pages, but should the reader be sufficiently interested, dozens of interesting examples of the exquisite needlework executed by our industrious ancestors will be found in the Victoria and Albert Museum.

1670—1680 (*continued*)

Gloves of an elbow length were again introduced about 1670 and worn on practically every occasion. The hood and mask still played an important part in every wardrobe, and the frilled beribboned " pinner " was first seen on these shores in the late 'seventies. Muffs, furs, sunshades, tippets —more often termed " Palatines "—painted fans, velvet shoes, long gloves, and embroidered stockings were all necessary etceteras.

The complexion received more attention than hitherto. Lily-white hands were acquired by the wearing of chicken-skin gloves at night. " Plumpers " were added to sunken cheeks, these were small balls of some flexible substance, jammed into the mouth, and poked up into the cheeks to give their wearers a youthful and chubby facial contour.

Many and varied were the styles in masculine head-gear, including the flat-brimmed, low-crowned beaver similar to that at the top of the opposite page. The high-crowned style with many feathers arranged at the back was the French mode, and not worn later than about 1672. Many varieties of the tricorn were also popular, and the fashion for turning the brim right back from the face and lining the edge with ostrich feathers was extremely prevalent.

1670—1680 (*continued*)

When Charles II's youngest sister arrived in England in the year 1670, she brought with her in her train the famous mistress of Louis XIV, Madame de Queraille. This beautiful woman wore her hair dressed in an entirely new mode —similar to that in the centre of the opposite page. The sides of the hair were curled and puffed and brushed out in a mass of small ringlets, whilst the centre parting and flatness on the top of the head remained in sharp contrast to the bunched sides ; the back hair was worn long, and drawn over the shoulders in several ringlets. Many pictures of the famous Court beauties have their hair dressed after this fashion—including Nell Gwynne.

The little lace caps were very fashionable. They were always adorned with a bow of ribbon in the front, and the hair was curled and cut so as to form a massive fringe of curls over the forehead. The back hair was drawn back and tied in a gigantic " boss " or bundle, called a choux. This was a very charming fashion, but seems to have been more in favour in France than in England. Madame Fontange wore the first top-knot ; which was named after her.

Lace veils were often worn over the head, and so were hoods. No method of hairdressing provided for ladies with straight hair, so the curling irons played a great part in the head-tiring of the time, and also the " Tour " or artificial bunch of curls on the forehead.

1680—1690

HERE is seen the amazing use of ribbon during the
'eighties ; dozens of yards must have been required
to tie the front of this lady's corsage, and hardly less to
decorate her swain's wrists, shoulders, hat, throat, sword,
and garters. The gown is made of flowered tabby and
decorated with fine black net lace. The gathered frill at
the feet was extremely fashionable, and so was the fringe
at the hem, or a deep band of inserted lace or embroidery.
Her companion is wearing a suit of black cloth, with a
flowered tabby vest and gold lace at the hands. His
"mouchoir" decorated with fine lace hangs gracefully from
his otherwise entirely ornamental pockets—"handkerchief"
was considered a vulgar word at this period ! The ribbons
on his coat are scarlet, also the dozens of buttons.

The daughter of Evelyn the diarist gives such a wonderful
description of the fashionable lady in her *Voyage into Mary-
land; or, The Ladies' Dressing-Room Unlocked*, that any other
description would seem futile. She satirically records the bare
necessities a wife will demand of her poor deluded husband :

" . . . Of Poïnt d'Espagne a rich Cornet,
   Two night-Rails, and a Scarf beset
   With a great Lace, a Collaret.
   One black gown of Rich Silk, which odd is
   Without one Colour'd, Embroider'd Bodice.
   Four Petticoats for Page to hold up,
   Four short ones nearer to the Crup :
   Three Manteaus nor can Madam lefs
   Provision here for due undrefs.
   Nor demy Sultane, Spagnolet,
   Nor Fringe to sweep the Mall forget :
   Of under Bodice—3 neat pair
   Embroidered, and of Shoos as fair :
   Short under Petticoats pure fine,
   Some of Japan Stuff, some of Chine.
   With knee hight Galoon bottomèd,
   Another quilted White and Red ;
   With a broad Flanders Lace below :
   Four pair of Bas de foy shot through
   With silver, Diamond Buckles too,
   For Garters, and as Rich for show.
   Twice twelve day smocks of Holland fine,

1680—1690 (*continued*)

With cambric sleeves, rich Points joyn
(For she despises Collertine).
Twelve more for night, all Flanders lac'd,
Or else she'll think her self disgraced.
The same her Night-gown must adorn,
With two Point Waistcoats for the morn :
Of Pocket Mouchoirs hope to drain,
A dozen lac'd, a dozen plain.
Three night Gowns of rich Indian Stuff,
Four Cushion-Cloths are ſcarce enough
of Point, and Flanders, nor forget
Slippers embroidered on Velvet. . . ."

Here is a glossary of some of the terms used above, with a few of the other quaint but interesting terms in use at the time :

Rayonne — Upper hood, pinn'd in Circle like the Sun-Beams.
Raggs — Names used for all sorts of Point Lace, etc.
Spannish paper — A beautiful red colour, ladies in Spain use
    for rouge.
Sprunking — A narrow sleeved gown.
Sultane — A gowne trimmed with buttons or loops.
Surtout — Night Hood covering the entire dress.
Pennache — A bunch or tassel of small ribbon.
Echelles — Stomacher laced with ribbons.
Campaine — A narrow picked lace.

One must visualize the dainty gentlemen of this time drinking chocolate, taking snuff, and nonchalantly combing their periwigs in public :

" . . . Fops and men of wigs and snuff,
    Knights of the famous Oyster Barrel Muff."

1 6 8 o—1 6 9 o *(continued)*

Muffs were worn by all fashionable gentlemen after about 1688–89. They were immense things, and attached to their wearers' waists by a wide belt and a large ring to which they were sewn. One of these may be seen on the page opposite.

The full-skirted coats were cut with a decided " waist," somewhat lower than the natural waist-line, and pleats or gores were inserted to give extra width to the skirts. The pockets which had originally served a useful purpose were now merely a place for added ornament and embroidery—frequently even these so-called pockets were non-existent, consisting of a band of some contrasting stuff or embroidery sewn on to the coat skirts, often only a few inches from the hem of the coat, and completely out of reach of the hands. Buttons were worn in large quantities on both vest and coat, and often the sleeves were decorated with them.

Breeches became tighter, and by about 1685 had ceased to be at all ornamental—in fact, they were no longer visible beneath the long-skirted coat. Stockings were worn drawn up over the knee and gartered just below ; sometimes two garters were worn, one above the knee and one below. Buckles on shoes took the place of the earlier bow or tie, and heels were worn even higher than during the 'seventies.

Flirting gracefully over a painted fan, their ladies also supped the fashionable chocolate or their cups of coffee. Their faces were patched, powdered, and rouged, and their hair arranged in a multitude of curls—each and every one with a different name. And piled upon their heads a variety of lace and ribbon conglomeration known as the " commode"—this will be dealt with later. So complicated was this " commode " that it attracted the jeering attention of every satirist and poet of the period. In her *Mundus Muliebris*, Evelyn's daughter remarks after a complicated description of head-tiring :

" Thus face that erst near head was plac'd,
Imagine now about the waist !

A passion for spot patterns, stripes, and plaids prevailed in ladies' clothes during the 'eighties and 'nineties, and fringe was used as an adornment to any garment. The " Echelles" or stomacher laced with ribbon was more fashionable than the plain bodice. Skirts became fuller as the period advanced towards the 'nineties, trains frequently being worn.

1680—1690 (continued)

No lady was seen abroad without her head dressed up in the most extraordinary manner. Patching was carried to ridiculous extremes—the mouche was often worn not only on the face but on the neck and shoulders. These patches were cut in a variety of shapes—stars, moons, etc., being the simplest and most usual forms.

One of the delightful satires of the period includes a minute description of head-tiring; unfortunately so much of it requires translation that a complete dictionary of the period is necessary. However, a small portion of these head arrangements will be found on the following pages, with a minute glossary for those who are interested :

> " The Settee, Cupée place aright
> Frelange, Frontange, Favourite,
> Monte la haut, and Palifade,
> Sorti, Flandan (great helps to trade),
> Burgoigne, Jardiné, Cornett.
> Frilal next upper Pinner fet . . ."

Pinner — A fan-shaped, pleated frill standing up in the front of the bonnet.
Settee — The double pinner.
Cupée — A special kind of pinner.
Frelange — The bonnet and pinner together.
Frontage — Top knot.
Favourite — Locks on temple.
Monte la haut — The wire to raise the head-dress.
Palifade — A wire sustaining the hair next the first knot.
Sorti — A knot of ribbons to be seen between the pinner and the bonnet.
Flandan — A species of pinner joined to the bonnet.
Burgoigne — The frill nearest the hair.
Jardiné — The single pinner next the Burgoigne.
Cornett — The upper pinner dangling about the cheeks.

Besides all this, the Palisade, though not decorative, served its purpose as a wire frame for holding up all this absurd affair ; the entire head-dress being called a Commode —which actually was a frame of wire, covered in silk, on which the head attire could be adjusted at once upon the head. The men's periwigs imitated the ladies' hairdressing in the two " horns " or curls directly over the forehead.

1690—1700

THE excessive ornamentation of ladies' attire may well be noticed on the example opposite. Gold braid and embroidery played a prominent part in decoration in the 'nineties. The sleeve, it will be observed, was no longer turned back into a cuff at the elbow, but often fell loose in a bell shape over the smock sleeve. The hair was often worn loose down the back, and especially by younger women, from about 1690.

In the example of men's attire it will be noticed that his cuffs are four deep. The excess of ribbons at this period was equal if not more than in earlier periods, though after 1692 only the scarlet bow was worn at the throat, the rest of the coat decoration relying on fur, braid, and embroidery. It should here be noticed how the cravat was wound around the neck and tied, hanging over the formal arrangement of ribbons. When untied, it was sometimes slipped through a button-hole on the coat, as illustrated on the next page.

The periwig no longer resembled the human hair, but was arranged in a mass of curls, those on the surface being cut at different lengths, to give the effect of ringlets all over. These locks were arranged in three or four separate bunches. Sometimes one mass behind and one over each shoulder, sometimes two at the back, as will be noticed on one of the previous pages—the back view of a gentleman in a black coat. The front of the wig was raised in two tufts over the temples, and the back of the head was left smooth to the nape of the neck, where the curls began.

Powder for the wig was introduced during the 'nineties, and although this method of hairdressing was not general for some years, there are many contemporary portraits of the periwig smothered in powder, and giving a greyish matted effect. A contemporary description of the youth who would be a gallant includes :

"A powder'd Wig, a Sword, a page, a chair,
  Learn to take snuff, drink chocolate and swear."

1690—1700 (*continued*)

The bustle in its first form was introduced about 1690.
The increasing tendency to bunch the skirts at the back
during the 'eighties eventually resulted in a roll of padding
round the back and sides of the petticoat, to give a yet wider
silhouette.   The bustle of the nineteenth century resembled
that of the seventeenth century in many particulars : the tight-
laced bodice and the frilled and ornamental petticoat was in
some cases almost identical with that worn by our own mothers
and grandmothers.   Some of the Parisienne fashion-plates of
this time might almost be those of the last century.

Ornament took on a formality similar to metal-work or
iron-work, and the embroidered waistcoat worn by the
ladies might almost have been a piece of armour so formal
was it.

I have purposely omitted the waistcoat from the last figure
on the opposite page, so that the knee-breeches may be seen.
This type was first worn in the late 'eighties, and by about
1695 the fuller ones had ceased to exist.   The skirt, it may be
observed, was still full, with large sleeves and frills at the
waist, the neck-line being brought right up to the throat and
finished with a tiny band or frill.   The cravat was often
several yards in length, of silk, linen, or lace, and the ends
always ornamented in some manner.

1690—1700 (*continued*)

In both examples of male attire on the opposite page, the long-sleeved waistcoat may be observed beneath the enormous cuff of the coat. The cuffs were more often than not well below the elbow after 1675. The first figure shows an exaggerated form of the curls over the temples. The ornate cuffs and pockets on this coat were decorated with black fur.

In Celia Fiennes' *Through England on Horseback*, there is an interesting description worthy of record of perhaps the earliest type of bathing suit : " The ladye goes into the bath with garments made of yellow canvas, which is stiff and made large with great sleeves like a parson's gown. The water fills it up so that it's borne off that your shape is not seen, it does not cling close as other lining." She goes on to say that the gentlemen wear drawers and waistcoats of the same sort of canvas. She also mentions in the same interesting, though monotonous, volume that Canterbury was a wonderful city with many French people, whose chief industry was silk-weaving. This silk-weaving must have been that alluded to at the beginning of this book.

Muffs and furs continued in favour during the 'nineties, the muffs usually being decorated with large bows of ribbon. The furs or palatines were always fastened with jewelled tags and clasps. The fashionable colour of fur included sable, ermine, and grey. Velvet scarves were often worn over the head-dress instead of the Rayonne.

1690—1700 (*continued*)

Every curl had its fashionable position and name. There were the Berger, Passague, Choux, Confidents, Cheve cœur, Cruches, and Frontange. The Berger was a plain small lock of hair turned up with a puff. The Passague was the curled lock at the temples. Confidets were the tiny curls near the ears. The Cheve cœur, or " heart-breakers," were the two small curled locks at the nape of the neck. Cruches were certain small curls on the forehead, and the Frontange was the top-knot—another fashion started by one of Louis XIV's mistresses—Madame Frontange.

※   ※   ※

Here, then, is the rough outline of costume worn during the reigns of the romantic Stuarts—from Elizabeth to Anne —from farthingale to bustle—from high-piled hair to stilted informality in head-dressing. One may see the man—his Elizabethan doublet changing for the high-waisted square-tabbed French one, then the loose waistless jerkin, the jackanapes coat of a hundred ribbons, and then eventually evolving into the skirted coats and waistcoats of the eighteenth century. His hair is worn increasingly long, and eventually unsatisfied with nature's gifts he adorns his head with a monstrous periwig ; this, in turn, elongating and becoming so large that no stretch of imagination could recognize it as a head of human hair. Foot-wear develops from a soft, slashed satin shoe, decorated with a satin rosette, to a ridiculously fantastic boot, cut, lined, and decorated to a point of absurdity, until it becomes a stiff, long, square-toed leather shoe, with a large lined flap over the instep, and decorated with buckles instead of ribbons. Breeches pass through numerous phases from the bombasted gathered stockings called farthingales by James I, to the tight-fitting knee-breeches of the eighteenth century ; taking in their stride the odd petticoat-breeches of the 'forties and 'sixties, the laced and ribboned affair of the Cavalier, the ugly plus-four-like calf-length breeches of the Roundhead fraternity, and the curious baggy, almost ankle-length frills of the late 'sixties.

And so we reach the end of a century full of new ideas, and holding far more variety in masculine attire than any other hundred years.

PART II

English Costume
of the
Eighteenth Century

FOREWORD

THE phrase " eighteenth-century costume " is one dear
to theatrical costumiers, and (although there has been
a very considerable diffusion of knowledge during the last
few years) it is still too often used as though the same clothes
were worn from 1700 to 1800. Eighteenth-century plays
are frequently dressed quite regardless of changes in fashion
throughout the century. Ramillies wigs are wedded to
1790 hats ; Louis XV. petticoats are worn with the towering
head-dresses of 1770, and Watteau gowns are matched with
toilettes of the French Directory.

That there is some excuse for this the following pages
bear witness. There is indeed a singular homogeneity about
the period, and when one considers that fashions came in
and went out more slowly than they do at present, that the
difference between town and country was more marked, and
that old people clung more affectionately to the modes of
their youth, there is perhaps less absurdity in treating the
century as one than might at first appear.

The present editor would be the last person to advocate
a pedantic archæological accuracy in reconstructing the
costume and background of the Comedy of Manners. There
is a sense in which the eighteenth century—if we forget the
revolutionary fervour of its close—was static, as timeless
and changeless as a Platonic Idea. The three-cornered hat,
the Watteau gown, the wig, the snuff-box, the shoe-buckles,
the knee-breeches, and the sword at a man's side—these are
surely Types laid up in Heaven.

The sixteenth century had been convulsed by the Reformation, the seventeenth by the Wars of Religion ; all was
confusion, all was flux. But in the eighteenth century the
surface of civilisation seemed to have set hard ; a culture
had been evolved which, however incapable of satisfying the
eternal needs of man, was, of its kind, perfect and complete.

That is not to say that it had no hidden misery and horror, no filth, no squalor, no sordid poverty. It had all these things; but it had also a Society, in the true sense, a European Society conscious of its unity and its common culture, and able therefore to devote itself to the elaboration of the elegancies of life, in a word to the evolution of Style. In nearly all the countries of Europe, Aristocracy had come to terms with Monarchy and had not yet been overwhelmed by the democratic flood. *Après nous, le déluge !* But till it came, the polite world enjoyed itself, and has left to future ages a complete picture of a homogeneous culture, a culture in which formal religion was tempered by scepticism and extravagance was restrained by taste, and in which two arts at least were brought to their perfection : the art of letter-writing and the art of conversation.

The calm was, of course, delusive, the seemingly solid surface scored with fissures and threatened with subterranean upheaval. Every age, no matter how static it may appear, is an age of transition, and the eighteenth century was no exception. Thought changed and fashion with it, and the century which began with Addison ended by accepting the extravagances of Rousseau. Costume is not a triviality ; it is the visible raiment of the soul. It is the purpose of the present book to display the slow but, in the end, considerable changes which affected European costume during the eighteenth century.

Color Plates for
Parts I, II, and III

1660
FRONTISPIECE (PART I)

1600–1610
(FACING PAGE 6)

1610–1620
(FACING PAGE 14)

1630–1640
(FACING PAGE 30)

1640–1650
(FACING PAGE 38)

1650–1660
(FACING PAGE 46)

1670–1680
(FACING PAGE 60)

1690–1700
(FACING PAGE 76)

1700
FRONTISPIECE (PART II)

1710
(FACING PAGE 96)

1720
(FACING PAGE 104)

1730
(FACING PAGE 112)

1740
(FACING PAGE 120)

1750
(FACING PAGE 128)

1770
(FACING PAGE 144)

1780
(FACING PAGE 152)

1836
FRONTISPIECE (PART III)

1800
(FACING PAGE 174)

1810
(FACING PAGE 182)

1820
(FACING PAGE 190)

1830
(FACING PAGE 198)

1840
(FACING PAGE 206)

1850
(FACING PAGE 214)

1860
(FACING PAGE 222)

1870
(FACING PAGE 230)

1880
(FACING PAGE 238)

1890
(FACING PAGE 246)

1900
(FACING PAGE 254)

English Costume
of the Eighteenth Century

1700

1700—1705

THE beginning of the century found the dress of Charles II.'s last years only slightly modified by the intervening reigns. James introduced no innovations, and the slight Dutch influence due to William III. only served to give to dress a certain stiffness and sombreness in keeping with the temperament of a King who cared nothing for the elegancies of life. Queen Anne, with whom the century opened, brought neither gaiety nor ostentation to a Court singularly lacking in both, and the dress of her period followed the rigid form of her predecessors. The main lines of costume, however, as it was to exist for nearly a century, were already decided, and this costume had certain strong characteristics which must be briefly considered.

The most remarkable of such characteristics is the wig. Wigs were worn in France very early in the seventeenth century, but did not reach England until the Restoration. Charles II. wore a voluminous black wig, and throughout his reign the wig fell on each side of the face with the ends drooping on to the chest. This proved so inconvenient, especially for soldiers, that the fashion arose of tying the hair back with a ribbon, and ultimately, of enclosing it at the back in a silk bag. But this, at the opening of the century, was still in the future. The cost of wigs was enormous, as much as £30 being frequently paid for a full wig of real hair. When one considers that this must have been the equivalent of at least £100 of our money, it is not surprising that footpads should make a first snatch at their victims' wigs.

Men's coats were so long that they almost concealed the breeches, and the waistcoats were almost as long as the coats. Shoe-buckles came in with William III., and were at first very small. They soon grew larger, and were often ornamented with jewels.

Women's dress was somewhat severe, although it had certain elements of informality. The small laced apron was much worn, even on important occasions. Below it was the flowered petticoat, much more important than the skirt, which was frequently drawn back in bunches or folds. The bodice of the dress, although cut low, was very stiff.

1705—1710

THE most striking thing about female costume at the beginning of the eighteenth century was the height of the head-dress. The fashion started in France when Mademoiselle Fontange, the King's mistress, finding her hair disordered while out hunting, tied it up with a ribbon. The fashion was followed, and formalised, so that soon an elaborate high lace cap stood on the women's heads, the hair being piled up in front and adorned with a wire frame covered with lace and ribbons. The Fontange head-dress was called a " commode " in England, and was seen as early as the end of James II.'s reign. It lasted throughout the reign of William and Mary, and, at the accession of Queen Anne, rose even higher. The lace used was very costly, for there was as yet no substitute for the real lace of Brussels and Mechlin except gauze, which did not give the same effect.

Men's hair was cropped very close, and in private the heavy full-bottomed wig was frequently discarded, an embroidered cap being worn in its place. Poets and painters are frequently represented in this curious negligé Waistcoats were still excessively long, and had to be left unbuttoned at the bottom in order to allow freedom to the limbs. Shirts were made of fine white lawn, with elaborate lace frills down the front and at the wrists. The cravat, which was also of lace, was one of the most costly parts of the costume. The sword was, of course, worn by all gentlemen, and had not yet assumed the dainty proportions of the dress-sword later in the century—a sword of the same size and shape as that which survives to-day in Court dress. Small boys did not wear a wig, but kept their own hair long in a kind of curly mop.

1700—1710

THE neckcloth, or cravat, had been worn by German troops as early as 1640, and, soon after the beginning of the new century, began to replace the lace collar in general use. It consisted of a strip of white material about a foot wide and a yard long, twisted round the neck and knotted in front. Considerable variety was practised in the manner of tying it, and each variety had a special name. A Steinkerk was a lace cravat tied very loosely, with the ends passed through a buttonhole in the coat. It was so called after the Battle of Steinkerk, where the French officers went into action so hurriedly that they had not time to tie their cravats properly; and the fashion was popular in England in spite of the fact that Steinkerk was an English defeat.

The large wig was worn by the wealthy, unconfined by any kind of ribbon or fastening, a fashion which must have been extremely inconvenient for those whose occupations involved rapid physical action.

The very short sleeve of Charles II.'s time had given place to a longer variety, with very elaborate turned-back cuffs, adorned with buttons and embroidery. Women's sleeves remained almost the same for many years. They were short, reaching to just below the elbow, and were finished with rather wide lace ruffles. Sometimes the lace was attached to the chemisette underneath, and not to the gown itself.

The odd habit of wearing patches on the face lasted almost throughout the century, and patches of different shapes and sizes were worn by women of all ages. Painting the face was freely indulged in, and the paints used sometimes contained chemicals very harmful to the complexion. The face was treated with wash-balls compounded of white lead, rice, and flour, with washes of quicksilver boiled in water, and with bismuth. This mattered less, perhaps, because women expected to look old in the early 'thirties.

1710

THERE is no very noticeable change in men's attire during the first ten years of the eighteenth century. Coats and waistcoats remained very long with large pockets in the flaps of each. The stockings were worn outside the breeches, drawn up over the knee, but gartered below. Stockings could be of coloured silk—blue or scarlet—with gold or silver clocks, but youths and poorer men wore black stockings of wool. In winter the curious fashion was followed of wearing several pairs of stockings at once.

In women's dress the fashions of the end of the previous century had been but slightly modified. The corset, which had reappeared about 1670, was worn very tight, and the bodice of the over-dress cut to fit exactly over it. It was laced from the bottom, with the effect of forcing the breasts upwards. Bodices were low, and a crimped frill was added to the upper edge—a survival from the lace collar of the previous age.

Already before the close of the seventeenth century gowns began to be looped up at the sides into *paniers*, and these *paniers* were superseded by hoops, which soon grew to enormous dimensions. The hoop was not, like the crinoline, an under-garment, but the outside petticoat itself stiffened with whalebone. The over-gown opened in front, and the petticoat was frequently of damask or other rich cloth. In winter petticoats were sometimes made of ermine, but, as by their nature, they were some little distance from the body of the wearer, they could not have made her much warmer. Petticoat, gown, stays, and cloak could be of different colours, but it was the petticoat which was usually embroidered and therefore formed the richest part of the toilet.

1710—1720

IN its earliest and most elaborate form the full-bottomed
wig was divided into three masses of curls, two in
front of the shoulders and one hanging down the back.
Above the forehead the hair rose into two peaks or horns,
sometimes exaggerated to grotesque proportions. However,
the fashion served to give increased height to the figure, and
a grave dignity to the face. A hat was completely unnecessary, and was often carried in the hand, but when worn,
had to be of considerable size. The back of the head was
smooth, the artificial curls forming a fringe at the edge of
the wig.

The hoop petticoat made its first appearance in the London
streets in 1711, and two English ladies, walking in the gardens
of the Tuileries in 1718, set the fashion in France. It has
been suggested that it came from Germany, from some little
Court where the great wheel farthingale known to Queen
Elizabeth and to Anne of Denmark had survived for more
than a century. The revived hoop was at its biggest in
England at the end of the other Queen Anne's reign.

The skirts of a man's coat were stiffened with wire to
make them stand out, but men soon abandoned the attempt
to compete with their wives in this particular.

Falbalas came in early in the century. These were crimped
or pleated flounces sewn horizontally round the skirt, and
were sometimes of a different material. This was not true
of *volants* or wide ruffles, which were assumed to be part of
the original dress.

The English corset was in general laced at the back, and
the whalebone stiffening went right round the body and
across the breast. The top edge was stiffened with a stout
wire, and in the lining in front a small pocket was contrived
to hold satchets of fragrant herbs. The French corset continued to be laced up the front.

1715

IT is often assumed that dress in the eighteenth century was very much more formal than it is to-day. In reality it was much less so, in the sense that considerably greater variety was permitted to individual taste, and that costume had not yet crystallised, as it were, into various accepted forms for different occasions and different occupations. An eighteenth-century gentleman would have been astonished at the uniformity of men's evening-dress, and even at the comparative uniformity of their everyday attire. Pages were not yet dressed in buttons, nor Eton boys in short coats and white collars. If lawyers wore full-bottomed wigs, so did every other dignified man. Lackeys wore the costume of the day with certain modifications ; there was even a certain amount of liberty allowed in officers' uniforms, and a definitely naval costume had not yet been invented. In particular, Court dress was simply the dress of the day, a little more elaborate and a little more costly.

Immense numbers of diamonds were worn both by men and women, for since the Dutch improvements in diamond-cutting at the beginning of the century, the stones could be made to present a much more brilliant effect than formerly. Diamonds were often borrowed or even hired for important occasions, such as Courts and weddings. The somewhat rigid bodice-fronts of this period lent themselves to the display of precious stones, and the stomacher was frequently embroidered all over with them, or else heavily laced with gold thread. Peers and Knights of the Garter and other orders wore their decorations even in the street, so that a man's rank could be easily recognised. We are still far from the days when it is considered bad form to wear even a miniature military ribbon. In this sense the dress of the eighteenth century was very formal ; and although the middle classes tried to ape the nobility, the high cost of the materials worn compelled them to keep at a respectful distance.

1710—1720

THE fashion for wearing the full-bottomed wig divided into three masses of curls did not last very long, owing to the growing consciousness of its inconvenience, even among the leisured.   Later, the wig was of equal length all round, but sometimes the portion at the back was divided into two, the ends being tied with ribbons.   This fashion persisted among old men until about 1760, but in general wigs became smaller about 1720, and continued to diminish in size throughout the century.

Cuffs were still large and sometimes heavily embroidered, but disappeared from hunting and riding coats.   Riding was also responsible for a modification of the coat-tails. These were buttoned back, and soon became merely ornamental, *i.e.* the revers were formalised as part of the decoration of the coat, thus making the wider opening at the front of the coat permanent.   The last vestige of this buttoning back is to be seen in the two black buttons in the small of the back of a modern morning or evening coat and in the more elaborate arrangement of buttons on the back lower edge of a soldier's tunic.

The most notable change in female attire is a lowering of the head-dress.   On the disappearance of the " commode " or Fontange head-dress, the hair was worn in a simple, almost negligent style, rather close to the head.   This fashion lasted, with but slight modifications, until the introduction of the towering head-dresses typical of the seventeen-seventies.   The habit of wearing caps, however, persisted, particularly in the middle classes.   These caps were usually quite small and perched on the top of the head, but were sometimes very rich, trimmed with fine lace, or made of lace entirely.   Servants' caps, or the caps worn by very old ladies and peasant women, are now the only survivals of this practice.

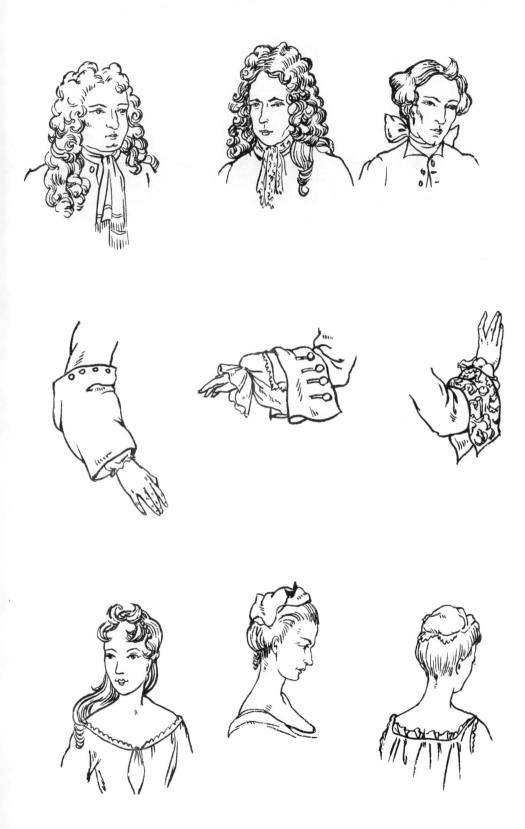

1720

AT the beginning of the century the increased facilities for trade with the East, due to the growing success of the East India Company, led to the introduction of vast quantities of Indian calicoes, which soon became very popular. English cloth manufacturers grew alarmed, and Acts of Parliament were passed, both by Queen Anne and George I., prohibiting the use of calicoes, silks, etc., from India, Persia, and China. These were, however, extensively smuggled, and Steele, in his plea for the weavers of England, gives an interesting list of the materials they had displaced : brilliants, pulerays, antherines, bombazines, satinets, chiverets, ora-guellas, grazetts (flowered and plain), footworks, coloured crapes (although most crape was made in Italy and was regarded by rigid Protestants as Popish), damasks, and worsted tammy draughts.

A wide over-dress came into fashion about this period. It hung loose from the shoulders and could be fastened down the front with bows of ribbon. This, which was called a *contouche*, was the equivalent of the modern *peignoir*, and at first was worn only in the house as a morning-dress, but soon became so popular that it appeared everywhere in the street. It could be made of silk, wool, or taffeta and some-times of light materials, such as gauze or muslin, worn over an under-dress of a contrasting colour. Its effect was one of charming negligence in attire, and is typical of the change which was taking place, less noticeably in England than in France, from the stiff formalism of the age of Louis XIV. to the rather frivolous elegance of the Rococo period. Men's coats were still rather sombre in hue, embroidery being reserved for the decoration of the waistcoat, which was often the most valuable part of the costume, unless the lace ruffles of the shirt were exceptionally fine.

1720—1725

THE seventeen-twenties were marked by the increasing popularity of the *contouche*, already described. It must not be thought, however, that the wearing of one of these loose dresses meant the abandonment of corsets. These formed an essential part of the under-dress, and were still worn very tightly laced in order to give a small waist to the figure, even when this was completely hidden by the full *contouche*.

Until about the year 1725, men wore on the right shoulders of their coats a number of bows of ribbon, the long ends of which extended to the elbows. These were a relic of the shoulder fastening which had been used at the end of the seventeenth century to secure the sword belt. Swords were now worn less conspicuously and sometimes discarded altogether except on formal occasions or for going about London by night, when the unarmed pedestrian was at the mercy of footpads and riotous marauders of all kinds. It was usual, therefore, to go to evening entertainments in the company of friends or servants.

Heel-making was a separate trade, employing a large number of hands, and this fact no doubt contributed to the persistence of high heels. The heels even of men's shoes were in general high, those of women extremely so. They were made of wood and coloured. In France, red heels were a sign of noble birth. The shape of shoes in general, even women's shoes, was somewhat clumsy, the heels being far too small and placed too near the middle of the instep. It would have been impossible to walk far in such shoes, and in the house women wore slippers.

For out of doors, ladies wore a long cloak with a hood attached to it. It was originally of scarlet cloth, and perhaps for that reason was called a " cardinal." It remained scarlet until the close of the century, when it became the fashion to wear black cloaks. It is interesting to note that the "cardinal" was the cloak worn by "Little Red Riding Hood " in the nursery story.

1725—1730

TRAVELLING cloaks for men were long and circular in shape, in fact they differed little from the *chlamys* of the Greeks (except that this was oblong), or the cloaks worn by Spanish peasants to this day. The appalling state of the roads in wet weather made high, stout boots essential, and these were of the pattern familiar from pictures of the Restoration period but with narrower tops, and, of course, unadorned with lace round the upper edge. For riding and travelling, women wore a modification of the male coat with turned-back sleeves and cravat, but their skirts were ill-adapted for any kind of exercise.

By 1730 the re-introduced farthingale may be said to have established itself, to last, with slight modifications, until the French Revolution. It grew to six feet in diameter and required an enormous quantity of stuff to cover it. At first, hoops of osier rods or cane were used, but these were superseded by the more reliable whalebone. The hoop was at first simply a cage—a series of hoops of different dimensions attached to one another by ribbons or strings at intervals round their circumference. About 1729 it became customary to cover this cage with cloth, with taffeta, and finally with silk, so that the hoop became a reinforced skirt. Sometimes in summer no other skirt was worn, and as the wearing of drawers was still very uncommon, the limbs were naked underneath the hoop except for the stockings which reached to just above the knee and were fastened by garters just below it. Hoops were violently denounced from the pulpit, but from any contest with the clergy fashion has always emerged victorious, and they continued to be worn even by servant girls, and by countrywomen going to market. Even the simplest *négligé* was duly provided with its framework of whalebone, and it became impossible for two women to walk abreast in the narrow streets or to occupy a carriage together in comfort. Even the staircases in private houses had to be provided with balusters curved outward in order to allow for the passage of the voluminous skirts.

1720—1730

B AG-WIGS were at first worn chiefly by soldiers, and when they made their way into civilian costume were regarded, in the beginning, as a kind of undress. The bag was made of gummed black taffeta, with a bow of the same material, and served to give an appearance of neatness without much trouble. The pig-tail was almost as popular as the bag-wig and for the same reasons of convenience. The *toupet*, or hair immediately over the forehead, was often natural, the join between the wig and the real hair being disguised by a liberal use of powder.

About 1730 the fashion arose of leaving the top buttons of the waistcoat unfastened in order to display the elaborately frilled shirt. This led to a modification of the neckcloth, which had shorter ends in order that the decorated shirt-front might be more easily seen. Sometimes the cravat with shorter ends was replaced by a neckcloth knotted at the back and kept in place in front by a jewelled pin. Military men wore two neckcloths one over the other, the under one of white muslin and that over it of coloured silk, allowing the white of the first to show between the folds.

Throughout the century, women's sleeves were almost constant in length, that is to say, the material of the dress reached just to the point of the elbow, and further length was given by two or three frills of lace. Although the elaborate " commode " had disappeared, smaller caps of lace were still worn in the house by women of all ranks and all ages. The styles of hairdressing varied considerably but within narrow limits, the hair being kept fairly close to the head. The necks of dresses were worn very low, in fact as low as a modern evening-dress, except that the opening was not so deep at the back.

1730

THE three-cornered hat, than which nothing is more typical of eighteenth-century fashion, was capable of a considerable amount of variety. Some hats were still laced and garnished with plumes like those of the previous epoch, but as the plume was worn on the upper brim, now bent inwards, it only appeared as a kind of fringe. Some hats were simply bordered with braid. The triangular form was kept by means of a cord, passed through holes in the brim and drawn tight round the crown, or else by a button acting as a kind of clip at the edge of the upturned brim. The earlier habit of festooning the hat with ribbons h ad been definitely abandoned.

The accession of George II. made very little difference to costume in England. The new king, like the old, was German, stiff in his manners and somewhat slovenly in his habits. His Court provided no centre of influence for the caprices of Society or the whims of fashion. Individual members of the aristocracy wielded far more influence than the Royal Family, and those who could afford trips to the Continent became, by natural consequence, the arbiters of taste.

Two accessories of costume in constant use were the snuff-box and the fan. The first was carried by every man, of every degree, and by many ladies. The smoking of tobacco was considered definitely " low," to be practised only by sailors and labourers, but vast quantities of the weed were consumed in the form of snuff powder, and every elegance of decoration was bestowed upon the boxes in which it was carried.

The fan was universal. In Queen Anne's reign it had been very large. Later, it became less pretentious and was decorated with painted scenes by the most able artists. Sometimes the paintings were designed to show political opinions. The material used was paper or, sometimes, thin white chicken skin, and the handles could be ornamented with jewels or enamels.

1730—1735

IN 1734 women's stays were worn extremely low. The bodies of gowns were laced up the front over a stomacher, or else stays were worn outside ; but in general there is little change in feminine costume since the last decade.

Men's costume also remained almost static, although the bag-wig was steadily ousting more elaborate types of coiffure. The turned back cuffs, frequently of contrasting colour to that of the coat, were cut in " pagoda " fashion, that is to say, narrow at the wrist and expanding sharply along the forearm. The name is a sufficient indication of the slight Oriental influence which made itself felt throughout the eighteenth century, not, however, so much affecting the shape of clothes as their colour, material, and decoration.

In France about 1730 men began to fasten their breeches at the knee over the stockings, but the older mode persisted among Englishmen for some years longer. The winter of 1729 was one of exceptional severity, and fine gentlemen, finding their thin stockings an insufficient protection against the cold, wore for a few months a kind of military gaiter. Men of the lower classes, with their grey or black woollen stockings, were better protected and had no need to adopt this short-lived fashion.

The fashion of leaving the waistcoat open in front in order to display the linen has been already mentioned. The custom reached its extreme in the early 'thirties. Sometimes, about a foot of frilled shirt was shown—a fashion to which the modern dress shirt and low-cut waistcoat can be ultimately traced. Women's riding-habits affected, as so often, a masculine mode, the waistcoat being shorter but of the same pattern, and the hat smaller but similar in shape to those worn by men.

Men's pockets were very ample and the folds of the long coat made it possible to carry comparatively bulky objects in them without spoiling their shape. Some fashionable gentlemen would carry a whole battery of snuff-boxes in the skirts of their coats.

1735—1740

THE arrival of Queen Caroline in England (for previously the Royal Court had remained in Hanover) gave a certain impulse to fashion, which had for some time languished without a leader. The Queen of George II. had a great liking for flowered silks, usually with a white ground embossed all over with a large pattern of gold, silver, or colours.

George II. himself had no pretensions to be a leader of fashion. His tastes were those of a simple soldier, and he had no feeling for any of the elegances of life. The ladies he honoured with his favour were neither beautiful nor elegant, and the English aristocracy went its own way, independent of the Court, adopting French fashions to its own slightly more rural use, but inventing little of its own. The prestige which English costume was to exercise all over the Continent was still more than half a century in the future.

Women of the middle classes still dressed with a certain austerity, although the wives and daughters of rich City merchants did their best to copy the fashions of St. James's. Some of the merchants themselves assumed, on Sundays, the fine coats and elaborate periwigs of the nobility.

Women's stockings, until the middle of the seventeen-thirties, were of all colours, green being one of the favourites. They were worked with clocks of gold, silver, or coloured silks. About 1737, however, there was a sudden rage for white stockings which greatly alarmed contemporary moralists. White stockings seemed to the preachers little better than nudity, but they continued to be worn until almost the end of the century. As a matter of fact very little of the stocking was seen, as dresses were never shorter in this period than to just above the ankles. Dancing or climbing into a coach may have revealed a certain amount of stocking to the eyes of the curious, but not enough, one would have thought, to alarm the most rigorous censor of morals.

1730—1740

IN addition to tie-wigs of many varieties there appeared, in the reign of George II., bob-wigs of various kinds. These imitated natural hair much more closely than the grand peruques ; they were worn by professional men, citizens, and even by apprentices ; lawyers affected a high frontlet and a long bag at the back tied in the middle, undergraduates a wig with a flat top to allow for the academic cap.

Cravats in this period show very few modifications ; in fact, although there were many varieties, each variety was almost as static as the modern neck-tie. The fronts and cuffs of shirts continued to be elaborately frilled. Coat-cuffs were wide and deep and sometimes heavily embroidered with silk flowers or with patterns in gold and silver thread.

There is little change to record in the forms of women's head-dresses. The ideal of the small, neat head was maintained ; caps became even smaller than they had been, and curls more neatly trimmed and arranged. The general shape of the female figure continued to be an equilateral triangle, resting securely on a wide base. The lower part of the body was inside the skirt rather than clothed by it, the only underclothes worn being in the form of a long " smock " or chemise. The evolution of underclothes should form an interesting and necessary chapter in the history of fashion. The phrase " body-linen " is still sometimes used, but actual linen underclothes must now be extremely rare. In the eighteenth century, however, linen was the usual material, very fine Dutch linen being imported for ladies' " smocks." Scotch or Irish linen could be bought for a third of the price, but was coarser and not so highly esteemed. Silk and lace-trimmed underwear was unknown in the eighteenth century.

1740

THE inconvenience of the circular hoop led to the introduction of one oval in shape, and much more graceful
in appearance. The materials, although not so heavy as
the brocades used early in the century, were very rich, and
often extremely costly.

An ingenious method was evolved (or rather revived
from the Elizabethan and Caroline periods) for decorating
women's dresses. This was the process of quilting which
had the added advantage, in winter, of making the clothes
much warmer. A layer of wadding was spread between
the lining (which had to be of linen or some equally strong
material) and the material of the dress, and was kept in
place by an elaborate stitchery pattern. Another method of
decoration was to cut out shapes of the same material as the
dress and to sew them on to it, having first inserted a stuffing
of wadding. These were known as " plastic ornaments."

As the century advanced, and the general prosperity increased, there was a gradual filtering down of luxury from
the aristocracy to the upper middle-classes. Working
people, especially in the large towns, often lived under
conditions which would not now be tolerated, but the
general standard of life rose steadily, until the set-back of the
Industrial Revolution.

The fine ladies of the period vied in extravagance with
their sisters on the other side of the Channel, and like them
adopted certain exotic modes intended to give them an air
of elegant eccentricity. The possession of a monkey or a
green parrot was a sign of luxurious refinement, and those
who could afford it went even further and purchased a little
black boy as a personal attendant. The presence of such a
slave, dressed in bright coloured and fantastic clothes, was
eminently calculated to set off both the toilette and the white
skin of his mistress.

1740—1745

IT should not be forgotten, in considering the costumes of a period as remote from us as the eighteenth century, that the tyranny of fashion was nothing like so complete as it is at present. Perhaps it would be truer to say that although fashion was tyrannical it was much less swift in its operation and, in the absence of fashion plates, a change in dress took much longer to filter down through the different strata of society. People in the country might well be twenty years behind the fashion, and the older men and women, even in towns, sometimes did not trouble to adjust themselves to changing taste.

In 1740, for example, it was quite possible to see an oldish man walking, even in the fashionable St. James's Park, in a large full-bottomed wig, while his son beside him wore one much smaller and neater. Older men clung also to their old-fashioned cravats, just as older men to-day wear the collars which were usual in their youth. There is perhaps no article of a man's attire about which he seems so conservative as his neckwear.

Women's dress shows certain modifications which must be briefly noted. The *sacque* gown, hanging loose from the shoulders and gathered in great folds over the hooped petticoat, appeared in 1740. It was another example of the general tendency to exalt the *négligé* into general wear. The effect could be charming, but involved considerable skill in dressmaking. Examination of the actual dresses of the period reveals the delicate cutting which was necessary in order to give the loose appearance at the back and yet mould the dress to the figure, for the falling folds were not added afterwards like a cape, but were an essential part of the back of the bodice.

1745—1750

THE loose *contouche*, already described, went out of fashion at the end of the seventeen-forties. Instead, there was introduced a gown or *robe ronde*, which opened from the waist downwards to display an underdress of the same material. In morning attire the place of the *contouche* was taken by various kinds of powder-mantles or dressing-jackets. The practice of powdering the hair demanded some kind of protection for the dress while the operation was being performed, and the toilette of a fashionable lady took up so much of her time and was attended, as a kind of informal reception, by so many of her friends (particularly men), that some kind of garment was necessary which was both warm and becoming. A woman of fashion was surrounded, from the moment she got out of bed, by a crowd of admirers, dressmakers, furniture vendors, musicians, dancing-masters, and dependents. Such a miniature court can be studied in all its detail in the well-known engraving by Hogarth.

Women's shoes were excessively flimsy and ill-adapted to any kind of hard wear. This fact receives interesting confirmation from a document, found among Lady Suffolk's papers, which gives details of the dress allowances for the daughters of George II. The provision was not on the whole extravagant, twelve pairs of thread stockings and two dozen cambric pocket-handkerchiefs being expected to last for two years, but a new pair of shoes, at six shillings a pair, was provided every week. Nine " day shifts " and nine " night shifts " were given to the princesses yearly, but the allowance of gloves rose to the astonishing annual figure of sixteen dozen pairs. It must be remembered, however, that in Royal households servants rapidly acquire a right to certain perquisites, and that articles of clothing were given away long before they were worn out. It was enacted, however, that the fine lace trimmings on the princesses' garments were not to be given away but saved for future use.

1740—1750

IN the early 'forties of the eighteenth century wigs became somewhat smaller, sometimes not touching the shoulders at all. By dandies they were sometimes worn exceedingly small, although satirical prints of the period probably overstressed their minuteness. The hat became smaller also, with very little border turned up to make the three-cornered shape. Cravats were smaller, and as this exposed more of the shirt, the front of this was more extravagantly frilled. The turned-down collar of the coat made an occasional appearance, as if in anticipation of the fashions at the end of the century, but this was unusual in the 'forties. Cuffs were still large but tended to be somewhat narrower at the wrist. Later in the decade hats were larger again, but wigs remained small, a contrast which had the effect of making the hat seem larger still.

Women still wore their hair somewhat close to the head, with one or two curls falling behind and others encircling the face. Caps were universally worn, sometimes approximating in shape to those worn by Mary, Queen of Scots, a lady to whom fashion has more than once returned for fresh inspiration. "Milkmaid" fashions for women had already made their appearance, and these involved country hats tied negligently under the chin with ribbons. Such hats are the remote ancestors of the nineteenth-century poke-bonnet. Throughout the eighteenth century colours had a political significance, and it is interesting to note that white hat-ribbons at this period denoted Jacobite sympathies. It is not always realised how much sympathy there was in England in 1745 for the attempt of the Young Pretender on the throne of his ancestors. If he had succeeded, the formalising influence of a German Court would have been removed, and English fashions would have been rapidly assimilated to those of the French, as had happened once before on the Restoration of another Charles Stuart.

1750

THE middle of the century marked what is perhaps the highest point of rococo style. The stiffness of the earlier years had been abandoned, and the extravagances of the 'seventies and the neo-classical negligence of the 'nineties were alike unthought of. The most typical characteristics of the century were at their most charming stage. The wig was neat and becoming. The three-cornered hat was of medium size—it had been ridiculously large in Marlborough's time, and became ridiculously small in 1790 ; coats and waist-coats were both dignified and graceful, the cut was good and the embroidery elegant. There was a tasteful moderation in the use of lace.

Women's dress was marked by a peculiarly charming form of the side *panier*, and was made of bright stuffs not too rich and heavy, for one result of the large *panier* had been to lead to the introduction of lighter and more flexible materials for dresses. In the late seventeenth and early eighteenth centuries very heavy stuffs had been worn, as these lent themselves to the somewhat rigid silhouettes of fashionable costume. The feminine frame, while capable of much in deference to fashion, cannot support an unlimited quantity of heavy brocade interwoven with metal strands. Some women managed to support damask, which is a heavy material, but looked well, with its bold patterns, when stretched over hoops ; but for the majority the result of the new modes was the introduction of lawn, muslin, and dimity, of simple texture but lively pattern, little bouquets or scattered flowers being the most frequent. The universal crinoline of a century later was to have a very similar effect.

1750—1755

THE year 1750 witnessed a striking decrease in the size of hoops, but the fashion for widening the skirt by the artificial aid of whalebone or osier rods was not to be abandoned for another generation, and in Court dress for another sixty years. The persistence and recurrence of hoops is one of the oddest phenomena in the history of fashion, and it is by no means absolutely certain, even yet, that they will not return. In 1800 it may well have seemed that they had gone for ever, but they had assumed their most extravagant form again in 1860, and that in the middle of the triumphs of the machine age, when the necessity of getting in and out of railway carriages might well seem to have made their use impossible.

Tight-lacing also, prevalent in 1750, was equally so a century later, and may come in again unless it is defeated by the modern enthusiasm for sport. Although it is always dangerous to generalise in questions of fashion, it may be said that tight-lacing is never very far away when the waist-line is normal. The only way to be certain of abolishing the corset is to push the waistline to just below the breasts, as was done during the first decade of the nineteenth century, or to lower it to the hips, as was the fashion about 1928.

The fullness of women's dresses during the early seventeen-fifties was reflected in the fullness of the skirts of men's coats. These, too, were sometimes stiffened with whalebone, or at least kept in place by pads, an odd example of the rare influence of feminine on masculine modes, since no man wishes to give the appearance of having full hips. In general, masculine fashions influence those of women far more frequently than feminine fashions influence those of men.

1755—1760

CONTRARY to the fashion at the beginning of the century, men's suits were sometimes made of the same elaborately patterned material throughout. This could be a cut velvet or an embroidered silk, and was naturally costly. The silk embroidery on men's coats sometimes involved months or even years of labour on the part of embroideresses, whose skill and taste have never been surpassed. Embroidered waistcoats were often the work of a man's wife or daughters, and making them served to pass the long winter evenings in an age almost devoid of outside entertainment.

Women's dresses were also sometimes embroidered, but relied more often on a woven pattern, or on tucks and flounces in the material itself. In the actual form of dress there was very little change, and in England at least, in the last few years of the reign of George II., there was no very outstanding example of feminine elegance to give a lead to fashion. What tendency may be traced was rather in the direction of simplicity, or what passed for such in an essentially artificial age when women took no exercise beyond a quiet stroll. Some gowns affected an air of elegant negligence by having neither bodice nor girdle, but hanging loose from the shoulders over the wide *panier*; others were fitted to the figure in front, but hung loose at the back. For this fashion heavy stuffs were unsuitable, so that dresses came to be made of lighter fabrics, such as lawn, muslin, or dimity, sometimes richly patterned, a tendency already noted as being due, in part, to the width of the hoops. The delicacy of the materials of dresses made some kind of protection from the weather doubly necessary. Cloaks with hoods were worn, and the sedan chair, for those who could afford it, saved the shoes of the ladies from being spoilt by the appallingly muddy streets. It is worthy of note that the umbrella first made its appearance in the London streets in 1756. It was carried by the philanthropist, Jonas Hanway, but his example was not generally followed for many years.

1750—1760

THE seventeen-fifties were a period of great importance in English history, and it is strange that the enormous military activity of the decade all over the world should have had so little effect even upon masculine fashions. The explanation, no doubt, lies partly in the fact that British victories took place for the most part in distant lands—at Plassey and at Quebec. Even the wars in Germany must have seemed sufficiently remote in that slow-travelling century, and although London swarmed with military men, especially in winter when the armies went into quarters, male fashion reflected the prevailing martial atmosphere only so far as to simplify the wig a little or give a military cock to the three-cornered hat.

On feminine costume the wars, unlike those of the Napoleonic era, left almost no trace at all, for the fashions were essentially feminine and so less susceptible than the revolutionary modes of the end of the century. It must also be remembered that the dress of soldiers was much closer in cut to that of civilians than during the days of the French Empire, when the fancy of military tailors was given full scope and the cut of uniforms decided for more than a century. Soldiers, in general, wore the civilian three-cornered hat, except that it was braided in a special way. Only grenadiers wore the mitre cap, and this was unlikely to be adopted for ordinary attire. The prevailing colour of British uniforms was already red, but the coats of civilians were frequently red also, and could be any colour. An officer was recognisable as such, but was by no means so conspicuous a figure in an ordinary crowd as a guardsman in full uniform would be to-day.

1760

A T the accession of George III., costume was, on the whole, simple, and the staid example of the Court did not tend to extravagance in dress. Hoops were still in use, but were of more reasonable size than had been fashionable a few years earlier. The small " gypsy hat " was worn even by the nobility. The gown was long-waisted and laced over the stomacher. Sleeves reached to the elbow, but full ruffles made them seem longer. Lace, in fact, was the chief extravagance, even the apron being frequently garnished with it. Handkerchiefs were frequently very costly, and more attention was paid to underclothes than during previous periods. Stockings were often white and made of silk and were fastened by garters, in general tied below the knee. Suspenders were, of course, impossible, as there was nothing to attach them to.

A *coqueluchon*, or small cape, covered the shoulders—a very necessary protection in cold weather, as bodices were somewhat low. Indeed, the high-necked bodice, even for day wear, is unusual until well on into the nineteenth century.

Children's costume, as such, had not yet been evolved, and boys and girls wore, with slight modification, replicas of their parents' clothes. Little girls, by modern standards, were far too heavily clad, and active boys were encumbered with long coats and three-cornered hats. In general, however, the costume of children showed, even as early as 1760, a tendency to simplicity and an adaptation to country usages, which gives it the appearance of anticipating the adult modes of the later century.

There is little hint in 1760 of the outbreak of fantasy in hairdressing which was to take place before the end of the decade.

1760—1765

THE end of the Seven Years' War made social inter-
course with France once more possible, and the
influence of French modes was suddenly renewed. French
hairdressers, milliners, and modistes arrived in London in
considerable numbers and found ready patrons among the
wealthy English aristocracy. Englishmen and women began
to pay visits to Paris and to bring new fashions with them
on their return.

Among other novelties was an adjustable farthingale.
This was an arrangement of hoops, or rather of iron ribs
encased in leather, and extending sideways from the waist
of the wearer in such a way that they could be raised at will.
In their normal position they extended horizontally outwards, the material of the dress hanging straight from them
to the ground, with the result that the skirt (if so monstrous
an object can be called a skirt), presented an oblong outline,
broader than it was high. The ingenuity of the new arrangement lay in the fact that the main bars of the structure were
hinged at the wearer's waist, so that the whole apparatus
could be raised at each side like the two halves of the Tower
Bridge, and so make it possible to pass through doorways
and narrow lanes. A modification of this fashion persisted, in
Court dress, into the nineteenth century.

Waists were very tight and long, with a pointed bodice,
often of satin, and cut very low. To protect the chest from
cold, a " breast-front " of lace and ribbons was worn, but
even with this, women's dress, even in the daytime, presented an aspect of *décolletage* somewhat startling to modern
notions. In winter small capes were worn as well as all-
enveloping cloaks, and in the early seventeen-sixties small
feather muffs were popular, both with men and women.
For the woman the muff also served in place of the as yet
uninvented handbag. When muffs grew larger people were
in the habit of carrying small pet dogs in them.

1765—1770

THE second half of the seventeen-sixties was a period of tranquil prosperity for England. The Indian and Canadian conquests had swollen the Empire to proportions undreamed of in an earlier age. The English colonies in North America, although restive, had not yet broken away, and the British fleet was supreme in the waters of the world. An enormous increase in commerce resulted, affecting fashion by the importation of foreign, especially Oriental, stuffs, and also by the new wealth, not only of the London merchants, but of the lately-arisen race of those who had made licit or illicit fortunes under the none-too-strict surveillance of the East India Company.

The current variations of fashion may be briefly noted. " Hats," says a contemporary writer in *The London Chronicle*, " are now worn upon an average six inches and three-fifths broad in the brim and cocked between Quaker and Keven-huller (*i.e.* the brims neither very loosely nor very closely attached to the crown). Some have their hats open before like a church spout . . . some wear them rather sharper like the nose of a greyhound. . . . There is a military cock and a mercantile cock, and while the beaux of St. James's wear their hats under their arms, the beaux of Moorfields all wear theirs diagonally over the left or right eye ; sailors wear their hats tucked uniformly down to the crown, and look as if they carried a triangular apple-pasty upon their heads."

The feminine coiffure, having been about the same for half a century, began to show signs of impending change. Already at the end of the seventeen-sixties woman had begun to abandon the small " head " and to pile the hair up from the forehead, in anticipation of the extravagant modes of the middle 'seventies. It was a definite breaking away from the close, simple hairdressing which had reigned supreme ever since the abandonment of the high Fontange or " commode " of lace and ribbon.

1760—1770

AS early as 1763 the Master Peruke Makers of London presented a petition to George III. in which they complained that gentlemen had begun to wear their own hair. The petition was without effect, for fashion is a heartless goddess and cares not how many honest tradesmen are ruined by her caprices. But the tendency was as yet little more than a tendency, and wigs continued to be worn by almost every man of any social pretensions for a generation longer. In 1770 there was a temporary fashion for round hats, forecasting the mode of the end of the century when the *tricorne* was definitely abandoned.

Innumerable varieties of neck-cloths were worn simultaneously, and there is little to add to what has already been said on the subject. Just as to-day one may see the " butterfly " collar, the " turn-down " collar, and the soft collar which is derived from it, wedded to bows and ties, so in the period 1760 to 1770 contemporaries were wearing lace cravats, neck-cloths fastening at the back, and the black ribbon " solitaire " fastened in front with a jewelled pin.

The three sleeves illustrated on the opposite page show varying degrees of elaboration but with an undoubted trend towards simplicity and the ultimate adoption of a purely formal turn-back of the cuff.

In 1760 powder was still worn, but women's hair was dressed rather simply, sometimes being drawn back from the face *à la Chinoise*, and surmounted by a small knot of coloured silk ribbon. Round the throat could be worn a ruche of the same material as the dress, and a fichu was draped across the shoulders not only for warmth, but as a necessary article of dress, for bodices were sometimes cut so low as to be hardly decent. Some kind of cap was almost universally worn, and could either envelop the whole head like a hood, surround the face with a fringe of lace, or rest daintily on the top of the coiffure.

1770

THE remarkable feature of the 'seventies of the eighteenth century was the size of women's head-dresses. The change had begun in the late 'sixties, from the " snug " hairdressing of the previous decade to veritable mountains of frizz, stretched over wire frames and sometimes sur-mounted by fantastic structures resembling ships or wind-mills or gardens. As few ladies had sufficient hair of their own to comply with the new fashion, false locks were added, wool was used to fill up the interstices, and the whole was then liberally greased with pomatum and heavily dusted with white or grey powder. The dressing of such " heads " was an elaborate and costly business, so elaborate and costly that ladies of limited means had the operation performed as seldom as possible, with horribly unhygienic results.

For men, the bag-wig was very fashionable, and round the throat, the solitaire, in place of a cravat, was increasingly popular. Dandies (although the name, if not the thing itself, is an anachronism) wore flower buttonholes, often of roses, renewed every morning, like the orchid of Joseph Chamberlain in a later age. The coat-cuffs were embroidered, and the buckles of the shoe set with precious stones or paste. The colours of men's clothes were brighter than they had been earlier in the century, but simpler in cut, with shorter waistcoats and tail-coats tending somewhat to the shape of the " cut-away." Coats for formal wear were elaborately and often beautifully embroidered, with sprays of silk thread flowers on the cuffs, round the seams, and on the tails. Button-holes became formalised, and collars were heavily decorated with needlework. Lace, however, was less in evidence as the century advanced, and as sleeves became longer and tighter there was less opportunity for its display.

1770—1775

CLOSE caps, resembling night-caps, were much worn in 1773, even in fashionable circles. Sometimes they had lace " wings " at the sides, giving a somewhat grotesque appearance to the head when seen from behind.

For a very short period men attempted to vie with women in the height of their head-dresses. The wig was built up with the aid of padding, or else rose steeply from the forehead in a kind of exaggerated *toupet*, with or without the support of a wire frame. As at the very beginning of the century when the full-bottomed wig had assumed such enormous proportions, it was now almost impossible for hats to be worn. The solution of the problem, however, was not, as it had been, to make the hat larger. On the contrary it became even smaller, and was never worn at all but merely carried in the hand and placed under the arm. Indeed, in polite society it became the masculine equivalent of the feminine fan.

This appurtenance of the toilet played a great part in eighteenth-century life. The rigid fan of the sixteenth century was an awkward engine compared with the graceful folding fan of the eighteenth. It could be carried easily, expanded quickly, and used both for cooling the face in the terribly overheated ballrooms of the period, and as an instrument of coquetry to add piquancy to smiling eyes, to conceal a blush, or to stifle a yawn. The mere fact that it could be folded within bone or ivory handles made it possible to use delicate materials such as silk or chicken-skin parchment, and to employ the best artists to paint exquisite little scenes thereon. Sometimes the fan, like the snuff-box, had a proper and a " gallant " side, either of which could be turned outwards at the will of the user. Some of the eighteenth-century fans which have come down to us are miracles of a delicate artistry which has never been surpassed.

1775—1780

THE head-dress of women reached its most fantastic height in the middle 'seventies; indeed, it almost seems as if the growing tendency for men to wear their own hair, or at least to combine more and more of their own hair with a diminishing wig, spurred the perruquiers on to invent even more elaborate head-dresses for women in order to keep themselves in employment. The dressing of a head for a fashionable function occupied three or four hours. With head-dresses of such enormous size it was essential for ladies to have hats to match, although sometimes a comparatively small hat was worn pinned firmly on top of the coiffure. Sometimes the hat was a part of the hairdressing, or, rather, the latter was so elaborate as to render a hat superfluous.

Bonnets of satin, taffeta, or linen were worn by women of all classes *en négligé, i.e.* on any occasion when full dress was not required, such as going to church or for a morning walk.

Long walking-sticks with gold or silver knobs were carried both by men and women, and the practice of wearing swords fell more and more into disuse, except among military men.

About the year 1778 a fashion arose of trimming the diagonal front edges of the overskirt with a frill of the same material as the flounces of the sleeves. The overskirt was sometimes puffed out with a stuffing of loosely crumpled paper which made a strange rustling noise when the wearer moved. The underskirt was richly ornamented either with horizontal gathers of its own material or with strips of lace, ribbon, or fur. The two skirts were frequently of contrasting colours or of lighter and deeper shades of the same colour. The skirt with *paniers*, before its final disappearance, was worn short, showing the shoes and the ankles, and, as always, a shorter skirt led to increased care for the neatness of shoes and stockings.

1770—1780

FROM the end of the seventeenth-seventies there is, quite suddenly, an enormous increase in the number of documents which may be consulted by the student of fashion. In a word, the fashion plate springs into being, and it is interesting to note that some of the earliest fashion plates were not concerned with the whole costume but with the method of dressing the hair. The fantastic hairdressing fashions of the decade made ladies all the more eager to be aware of the latest mode, and the engravers and publishers were not long in satisfying their curiosity.

A publication with the interesting title of *Souvenir à l'Anglaise et Recueil de Coëffures* appeared in Paris in 1778, and there was soon a rage for such aids to modernity on both sides of the Channel. The fashion paper was fairly launched and no doubt contributed largely to a more rapid changing of modes than had been customary or, indeed, possible earlier in the century. It is probable that the vogue for caricatures may have contributed to the same effect, for by exaggerating each fashion in turn and so tending to make it ridiculous, the growth of new fashions was stimulated. In England, however, the great growth of fashion plates belongs rather to the turn of the century than to the decade now under discussion.

Masculine hairdressing became neater and closer to the head, the three-cornered hat being very small and worn far forward, so that the brim came just above the eyes. Sleeves were sometimes extremely narrow, with a simple edge of lace protruding from the cuff. The formalised buttons and buttonholes, which had once had the genuine function of keeping the turned-back cuff in place, remained on the sleeve as decoration, just as they have remained to this day, sometimes as many as four, sometimes one, but never entirely absent. The *vestigial* element in dress is always large and is a proof of the extraordinary conservatism of fashion beneath all its apparent change.

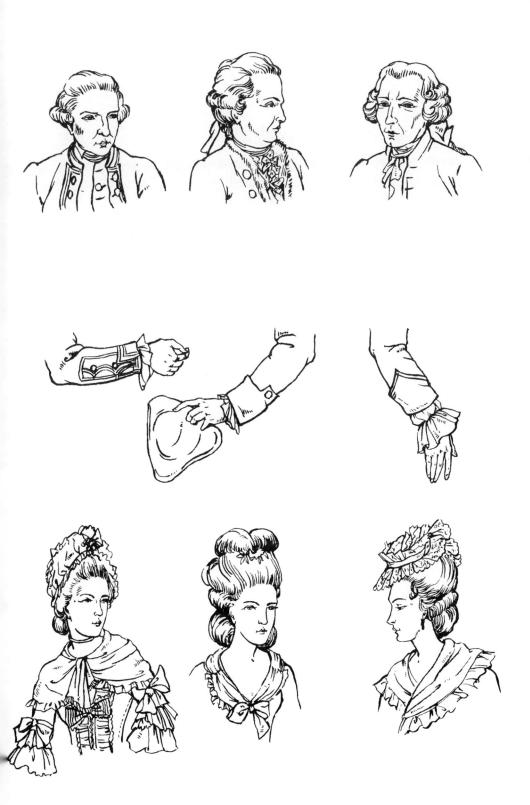

1780

BY the year 1780 the revived farthingale or hoop may be said to have disappeared, its place being taken by small pads or cushions fastened to the hips, and then by a single pad at the back. In fact, the eighteenth-century equivalent of the crinoline was followed by the eighteenth-century equivalent of the bustle, although neither of the names had as yet been invented. The recurrence of fashion is an attractive theory, but such recurrence obeys some peculiar rhythm of its own, so that prophecy becomes difficult if not impossible. There is, none the less, a certain parallelism between the course of fashion in the eighteenth and in the nineteenth centuries, even in small and seemingly unimportant details.

The fashion of embroidering men's coats all over their surface had now been abandoned. Even waistcoats were not so highly ornamented as they had been, the embroidery being now generally confined to the skirts, the pockets, and the buttonholes.

There was a reaction against high heels and a forecasting of the almost completely heelless shoes of the early nineteenth century. Improvements in the craft of shoemaking made all shoes much more comfortable, so that the use of house-slippers was abandoned. The long tongue of the upper disappeared almost completely.

For women, the large horizontal hat, usually worn at an engaging angle and adorned with ribbons or feathers, began to be fashionable in 1780, or soon afterwards. The material of these hats was straw or silk or some light foundation, and it was securely fastened to the coiffure with pins to prevent it from falling off. Even so it must have been no light task to manage the head-dress of the period in a high wind. Men were beginning to grow tired of the universal *tricorne* and to cock their hats in a different way—straight up and down at the front and back, so that the two edges lay together. The hat thus treated was the ancestor of all the " Napoleonic " hats and of the cocked hats of modern admirals and generals.

1780—1785

ABOUT the year 1780 there was a wave of simplicity, not the real simplicity of the time of the Revolution, but a pseudo-pastoralism derived from the example of Marie Antoinette at the Trianon. There the ladies of the Court played at being shepherdesses and dressed their hair in " milkmaid " or " peasant " fashion, but dresses were no less costly for being pastoral or pseudo-pastoral. The influence of the country was more effective in England, where there was a real enthusiasm for rural life and where men, at least, wore clothes suitable for hard weather and boots adapted to the muddiness of the roads. Some women, finding a semi-masculine riding-dress becoming, adopted it for morning wear whether they intended to ride or not. The bodice was made in imitation of a man's coat and waistcoat with overlapping revers, and the skirt was full, but simple and without trimming. On ordinary dresses trimmings were abandoned in favour of ruches of muslin or lace, arranged in flounces and sewn to the edge of the dress. Gowns were worn rather long, and the white stockings were invisible. About the year 1783 there was a rage for decorating dresses with straw, even men's waist-coats being ribbed with it, and straw coats, called *paillasses*, were worn by women.

About 1780 hats began to be perched on the top of the high coiffures, with the result that the head-dress itself grew smaller to accommodate them. Hair was crimped and arranged in " hedgehog " fashion, puffed out from the face, and hats had to be very large in order to cover it without spoiling the effect. Some of the mob-caps of the period were almost as large as hoods and, indeed, resembled them very closely. On more formal hats there was a rage for ostrich feathers, a fashion immortalised by Gainsborough in his portrait of the Duchess of Devonshire.

1785—1790

TOWARDS the end of the 'eighties it became the fashion for women to wear a separate jacket-like garment called a *caraco*. This was close-fitting and made in a masculine style. Beneath it a tight-fitting dress was worn, bodice and skirt of the same material, the skirt contrasting with the *caraco*, which came more than ever to resemble a man's dress-coat. Sometimes the under-dress was without a bodice, a light corset being worn in its place, concealed by a kind of front or stomacher, made to resemble a man's waistcoat. This very masculine attire was sometimes worn with a large apron with pockets.

In winter *mantelets* were worn. These were short capes of silk occasionally edged with fur. When fitted with wide, half-length sleeves, the winter garment was called a *pelisse*.

From 1786 there was a fashion for beaver hats similar to those worn by men, but more richly trimmed.

The three-cornered hat may be said to have disappeared after the French Revolution. Shoe-buckles also fell out of fashion, being replaced by shoe-strings, although the growing use of boots rendered both unnecessary.

The heels of women's shoes were lower than they had been throughout the century, and the upper was more open, ending a couple of inches behind the toes. Shoes were more comfortably made, with the result that walking became more fashionable.

Swords, which had been worn throughout the century, disappeared about 1786, except with Court dress. About the same period, the wide skirts of men's coats gave place to long tails. Coats were double-breasted and very short in front, so as to reveal the waistcoat. In 1790 there was a temporary fashion for black coats, but the breeches and waistcoats remained brilliant in colour. Waistcoats and stockings were ornamented with vertical or horizontal stripes.

1780—1790

THE collars of men's coats, non-existent in the earlier part of the century, could be worn turned over in the modern fashion or else standing rigidly round the neck. The space between the neck and the collar was filled with a scarf wound several times round—the ancestor of the modern neck-tie. This neck-scarf was often of muslin, as its predecessor had been of cambric. Sleeves became still narrower and very long, so that little of the fine frills at the end of the shirt sleeve could be seen.

One of the fashionable methods of dressing the hair was to have two or three horizontal curls at the side and a little formal queue at the back. This mode has persisted, in a smaller, somewhat stylised form, in the barristers' wig of to-day, so that while the judge on the bench wears a wig dating in shape from the beginning of the eighteenth century, the wigs of counsel date from about 1780. State coachmen's wigs, worn by the coachmen of the nobility until the beginning of the twentieth century, date from the same period as those of barristers.

The typical head-dress of the seventeen-eighties for women tended to width, just as that of the 'seventies had tended to height. The effect was somewhat suggestive of the loose hair of a cavalier during the reign of Charles I. Over the hair large mob-caps could be worn, or else a broad-brimmed straw hat very simply trimmed. The general appearance could be charming. The hair, except on formal occasions, was worn without powder, but curling was essential if only to expand the hair to the required size. A kind of hood made of crape was very fashionable, and as the hair completely filled it, it was impossible to tell whether it was a hood or a cap. In winter hoods were edged with fur. Caps persisted for many years, and certain combinations of black and white lace remained as an old lady's head-dress in remote places for nearly a century.

1790

IN masculine attire the beginning of the seventeen-nineties marked the victory of English modes over French ones, and the beginning of a dominance which they have maintained ever since. The " European dress " established at the beginning of the century by the prestige of the French Court now gave place to a coat recognisably similar to that worn to-day in evening-dress.

The cut of the masculine coat had been fixed for so long that it must have seemed difficult, if not impossible, to change it. Ever since the evolution of coat and waistcoat at the end of the seventeenth century, the relationship of these two articles of attire had been constant. Now some genius adapted the double-breasted coat from the English riding-coat with its two rows of buttons, and two far-reaching consequences immediately followed, both caused by the necessity of keeping a double-breasted coat fastened if it is to preserve its fit. Had the coat been as long in front as formerly the wearer would have been considerably hampered in his movements, and the waistcoat—which had always provided an opportunity for the display of the wearer's taste—would have been totally concealed. Thus tailors began to experiment by cutting the front of the coat away. The period also witnessed an orgy of " revers," even waistcoats being provided with them, often of a colour contrasting with those of the coat.

As the waistcoat pockets were no longer easily accessible, it became the fashion to wear the watch in a front pocket of the breeches. Sometimes both front pockets carried a watch, with seals dangling down outside. The remote successors of these dangling seals were worn into the twentieth century, and may still occasionally be seen, but as the trousers have no front pockets, the " fob " is fastened to the braces.

1790—1795

DURING the early days of the Revolution in France, and most of all during " the Terror," it became positively dangerous to be seen in the streets of Paris in rich clothes. Not only was the cut plainer, but the materials also. Silks and satins disappeared, their place being taken by cotton, Indian print, and lawn. In England, there was less reason for change, not only because of the stability of the Government, but because the English gentleman with his country habits wore, by preference, clothes much less gaudy than those of his French counterpart. From one point of view, the Revolution was a victory for English fashions, even in France. The top-boots, the unembroidered coats, the stout breeches made for much hard wear in the saddle, passed from the country into the town, and men entered drawing-rooms in costumes more suited to the hunting-field. But Englishmen never adopted the extremely high and voluminous neck-clothes which in France actually rose to cover the chin and sometimes the mouth. A short bamboo cane or riding-whip replaced the long walking-stick of a few years before.

In women's costume, England almost entirely escaped the worst extravagances of the French *merveilleuses*, who went about the streets of Paris in a costume supposed to be Greek, consisting of one semi-transparent chemise-like dress with pink skin-tights worn underneath. The girdle was placed immediately under the breasts, and this fashion reached England towards the end of the century, when very high waists came into fashion. The rage for tall feathers also came from France—a little late, for they had been introduced by Marie Antoinette. It is curious to reflect that the custom of wearing two feathers upright in the hair, which began in this period, has lasted, in Court dress, until our own time.

1795—1800

IN the middle 'nineties, or, in extremely fashionable circles, just before, the short waist became the rage. The waist, in fact, slipped up to immediately below the breasts and remained there for about twenty years. The materials used for dresses were very thin, but unlike those employed in the days of *paniers*, they were neither used in great quantities nor elaborately patterned. Simplicity was pushed to the verge of indecency, although the transparent dresses worn in France were never popular in England. We have seen that at the beginning of the century English manufacturers were complaining of the importation of calicoes from India; now, owing chiefly to the invention by Arkwright of the spinning frame, the position was reversed, and the East India Company was driven to complain of the harm done to its import trade by the successful manufacture of British cottons and muslins.

The scantiness of dresses led to the popularity of large fur muffs and to the introduction of wraps, cashmere shawls, or sometimes mere handkerchiefs disposed like a fichu to protect the throat. A short, close-fitting coat with long sleeves, called the spencer, appeared about 1797.

In thin and unvoluminous dresses with no under-petticoats, women, at the end of the eighteenth century, found themselves confronted by a new problem—that of pockets. Their absence led to the invention of the reticule or handbag. It was much laughed at, but has survived several periods of eclipse, to become, in our own day, the most necessary accessory of female costume.

High-heeled shoes began to be discarded in favour of coloured slippers, made of satin for evening wear and of Morocco leather for day-time. They were extremely flimsy, for only eccentric young women, like Wordsworth's " dear child of Nature," went for long walks in the country.

1790—1800

IN 1795 Pitt imposed a tax on hair-powder, and so almost
extinguished a fashion which was already on the wane,
although true-blue Tories still continued to wear both wigs
and hair-powder as a patriotic gesture, and to distinguish
them from those who sympathised with the French Revolution.   Political opinions sometimes decided the colour of
a man's clothes.   The Tory supporters of Pitt wore scarlet
waistcoats, while the Whigs who supported Fox wore
yellow.   The partisans of Fox had also the very odd habit
of carrying large red-fox muffs.

Sleeves became simpler than ever, the turned-back cuff
being altogether abandoned, or else symbolised rather than
imitated by a band of braid.   The number of buttons worn
on sleeves was also noticeably reduced.

About the year 1795 caps were discarded in fashionable
circles in favour of bandeaux or fillets in supposed imitation
of classical models.   These fillets were made of muslin or
of strips of coloured embroidery.   Very few English women
in these years of hostility to France followed the French
fashion of having their hair cut short at the back and hanging
in dishevelled locks over the face, à la Titus.   A few may be
noticed, however, particularly in the charming stipple engravings of Adam Buck.

From 1794 to 1797 there was a fashion for enormous
ostrich plumes in the hair, sometimes two or three of different
colours being worn together.   The plainness of the dress
of the period seemed to demand the wearing of jewellery,
but as diamonds and other precious stones were temporarily
out of fashion, semi-precious stones and corals were fashioned
into cameos in imitation of the antique.   Everything, in
fact, was antique or pseudo-antique, and the century which
began with the stiff splendour of the *Grand Siècle* ends in an
orgy of the neo-classical.

PART III

English Costume

of the

Nineteenth Century

FOREWORD

IT was in the Nineteenth Century that the Modern World took shape, and it would be strange indeed if the political and economic revolutions which determined the history of Europe during that hundred years should have found no reflection in the evolution of our clothes. In their hatred of the embroidered garments of the nobility, the men and women of 1789 turned, on the one hand, to English country fashions, and, on the other, to what they imagined was the clothing of the Ancient Greeks. The result was that top-boots for men and a single, flimsy, chemise-like garb for women became the accepted wear. Men abandoned knee-breeches, long flapped surcoats and wigs ; women gave up loops, brocade and the use of powder on the hair. But the greatest revolution of all was that henceforth the classes could no longer be distinguished by striking differences of dress. Yet changes in fashion, especially for women, happened all the more frequently, for only by adopting the very latest novelty could the woman of wealth distinguish herself from her sisters. For a whole century the accepted forms of male and female costume had remained fundamentally the same. Once the tradition was broken, anything might have happened. What actually did happen, and how we arrived by easy stages at something approaching the dress of to-day, it is the purpose of the following pages to show.

J. L.

1836

1800

IN the time of the French Directory, during the first flush of freedom from the old eighteenth-century modes, women's dress had pushed daring to the point of indecency, and men's, with its immense tails and prodigious neckcloth, had been more fantastic than the style it had superseded. But by 1800 sobriety had won its victory. Feminine dress was still in one piece, divided into skirt and bodice by a cord or ribbon tied immediately under the breasts. A short jacket was sometimes added as a protection against the cold—a protection much needed, as the garments of the day were scantier even than those of modern times.

The materials used were excessively light muslin, batiste, lawn—and the caricaturists made merry over the disasters of revelation consequent upon the slightest sudden shower. Gérard's painting of Psyche set a fashion for white dresses which was very generally followed. The wild hair of 1794 had been drawn closer to the head, but it was still short both for men and women. Men's coats had assumed the cut-away shape which persists to-day in formal evening and morning dress. Their neckcloths had shrunk to moderate proportions and the beginnings of the modern bow-tie were apparent. Breeches had not yet been entirely abandoned, but were already on their last legs. The three-cornered hat with plumes had disappeared, and the ancestor of the silk-hat was already taking shape.

1800—1805

SOON after the beginning of the century, women began to be bored with the single garment, and to wear over it a second, cut open in front or short in the form of a tunic. The romantic elements of the late eighteenth century began to break through the pseudo-classical crust, and dressmakers began to puff the sleeves in the manner of the Tudor period and to encircle the neck with the beginnings of a high lace frill. Already in 1801, ruffs made of Brabant lace, and called " Betsies," after Queen Elizabeth, had made their appearance, and although the high waist continued, revolutionary simplicity was gone for ever. The poke-bonnet, which was afterwards to attain to such formidable dimensions, had been known as early as 1797, and by 1805 had begun to be common.

Men's hats, in that warlike age, were sometimes cocked in the military or naval fashion, but the high-crowned beaver was already winning its way to universal acceptance. In masculine clothes the ascendancy of Brummel was establishing the reputation of English tailors for fineness of cut which has persisted until to-day. An ideal of cleanliness was adopted both of the clothes and of the person, which is one of the debts which the modern world owes to the early nineteenth-century dandy.

1805—1810

AFTER 1805 the new style may be said to have become
established. The dress fitted closely, but no longer
trailed on the ground as before. The train of the early years
of the century was abolished, and the skirt began to be
worn shorter. By 1808, in some garments at least, the
feet were free, and two years later ankles were visible. The
shawl had made its first appearance in England as long ago
as 1786, but it became the rage during the first ten years of
the new century. The passion for " draperies " encouraged
the use of shawls, and cashmere became extremely fashionable. Even the introduction of fur cloaks from Vienna
about 1808 failed to displace the shawl, and it continued to
be worn until quite late in the century. Nothing in women's
dress, however, was of such importance as what was hap-
pening to men's—the triumph of trousers. Originally the
costume of the English sailor or the French *sans-culotte*, they
gradually made their way into the most fashionable society.
Soon only elderly men were to be seen wearing breeches,
and after Waterloo they may be said to have disappeared
from ordinary attire.

1800—1810

THE first ten years of the century witnessed, as we have seen, the beginning of the poke-bonnet, and the development of men's linen and neckcloths along the lines they have followed ever since. The frilled shirt, allowed to project through a very low-cut waistcoat, became the ancestor of the modern evening-dress shirt, and it is curious to note that the soft shirt with many pleats, which made its appearance after the European War, was in reality less of a novelty than a revival.

Hair, which about 1798 had begun to be cut quite short, was, in the early years of the new century, brushed forward over the eyes. By 1809 it was the fashion to curl it, and shortly afterwards was adopted the plain short cut which has existed, with minor modifications, ever since. Women's hair began to be worn longer.

1810

THE general dress of the day was plainer, both for men and women, than it had been for centuries, but ceremonial dress was still worn at the English Court, and Napoleon re-introduced it into his own. Indeed, in spite of the war against England, the winter of 1809–10, just before Napoleon's second marriage, was the most brilliant and extravagant season of any that had been seen since the fall of the *ancien régime*. Men's fashions had firmly adopted the English mode, but women's continued to be inspired by Paris. The turban, which is said to have been inspired by the campaigns in Egypt, had become a recognised item of feminine attire. Stays came in during the winter of 1809 and persisted for a century.

1810-1815

EVEN in winter, morning dresses continued to be made of muslin, although bombazine (then considered a very elegant material) was also worn. Dinner dresses were made of velvet and satin. Velvet frocks trimmed with swansdown were popular about 1812. Collars, for day wear, became noticeably higher, and short sleeves disappeared. In the evening, gowns were cut square over the bosom and very low. Shoulder straps entirely disappeared. Dresses were trimmed with frills or rolls of the same material, and it was not until 1812 that different coloured trimmings began to be used. The article of attire most characteristic of the period was the pelisse, a kind of over-dress, buttoning down the front, and sometimes made fairly short in order to show nine or ten inches of a white muslin dress underneath. In very severe weather a " pilgrim's cloak " was thrown over the pelisse. Furs also were worn in cold weather, and ankle-boots for women made their appearance. They were almost heelless, but still pointed, and sometimes laced behind. Slippers had slashings of contrasting colours. Gold ornaments began to replace the coloured stones which had previously been popular.

In men's dress, trousers are seen to have won their triumph, and the astonishing reign of the tall hat has been successfully inaugurated. Some older features of dress, however, still persisted, notably the coat with many overlapping capes, which survived among coachmen even later. Waistcoats once more came down to the hips.

1815-1820

THE beginning of the long peace marked a considerable change in the general shape of women's dresses. The waist became even shorter than it had been before, and the skirt descended from it in straight lines to just above the ankles. The bottom of the skirt, however, was very much wider and much more decorated, generally with somewhat stiff *rouleaux* of material—a kind of incipient (and external) crinoline. The use of transparent materials worn over opaque ones began to be appreciated, and it became fashionable to wear a frock of pink crape over a slip of white satin, or a dress of net (the name " patent net " shows how recently it had been invented) over a slip of coloured satin or sarsnet. Sleeves became very elaborate, and the exaggeration of the shoulders foreshadowed the fashions of the 'thirties. Puckered muslin was used to give to sleeves the puffed appearance of the time of Henry VIII, and the Tudor ruff round the neck emphasized the period from which dressmakers were drawing their inspiration. The influence of Scott was also to be seen in the fashion for plaid scarves and sashes, which were very popular about 1817.

Men's fashions exhibited no change worth recording.

1810-1820

THE military enthusiasms of the time are seen in the adoption for women's dress of details from soldiers' uniforms. Even the forms of headgear were copied, and froggings and epaulettes gave an added touch of patriotic fantasy. The so-called Wellington hat, the Wellington bonnet, and even the Wellington jacket (made of twilled sarsnet and worn for dinner parties) were extremely popular. There was also a Wellington mantle, like a small Spanish cloak, and it is sad to think that the name of the great soldier, having rested lightly for a moment on so many articles of attire, should, in the end, have clung only to boots.

What was known as the plain cottage bonnet became somewhat more elaborate, being cut out in front so as to display a lace cap underneath. Hats became higher and were decorated with flowers, feathers, or bands of plaited " grogram " or puffed gauze. At this period, and much later, hats were worn in the evening with everything but full dress, for which flowers or feathers were substituted.

Ostrich plumes became fashionable, and, worn upright in the hair, they have persisted for court dress until to-day.

Men's collars continued to be high, and the neck-cloth was still voluminous.

1820

ALTHOUGH white was still fashionable, coloured dresses were sometimes worn, and, as a somewhat daring innovation, a coloured bodice with a white skirt. The waistband, which was occasionally coloured even when the dress was white, sank to its normal position immediately above the hips. Sleeves continued to be puffed and slashed in a pseudo-Elizabethan style. The hat was large, and plumes, sometimes of various colours, were much worn.

Drawers, long, tight-fitting, and trimmed with lace, began to be worn by women, although they were not universal until the 'thirties, or later. Little girls also wore them long, so that they protruded several inches below the skirts, and, had they not been so elaborate, would have looked like trousers. Sometimes these " pantalettes " were false, being merely attached by tapes above the knee.

Trousers for men were by this time almost universal, their supremacy never to be disputed until the coming of knickerbockers at the very end of the century. The tall hat was broad-brimmed, with the crown wider at the top than at the bottom. The collar of the shirt rose almost to the sides of the mouth, and the front of the shirt was frilled and allowed to protrude through the waistcoat.

1820-1825

LITTLE change was seen in women's dress during the early 'twenties. The waist remained high and bodices, which were very short, had a *bouffant* drapery over the bust, sometimes made of silk netting, to give (in the words of a contemporary chronicle) a fullness where nature had been less prodigal. Ball dresses were short, and the padded *rouleau* at the bottom gave them that weighted appearance so typical of the period. They were made of striped crape, flock gauze, rainbow gauze, plain *barège*, silk or tulle. Colours were tender rather than violent, the favourites being lavender grey, pale yellow, mignonette-green, and rose. Scarlet ball dresses were, however, not unknown. Hats were large and elaborate, being lined with velvet and trimmed with large plumes. There was a passion for feathers, and they were considered essential even on " satin bonnets for the morning lounge." Trimmings were sometimes of polished steel. Turbans of figured gauze were the favourite head-dresses of married ladies of middle age. For evening wear they were adorned with a few pearls or, in mourning, with a bandeau of jet or bugles, and a plume of feathers. Young ladies wore wreaths of flowers made of crape.

For men, the fit of clothes became even more important than it had previously been. The tails of a dress-coat were now cut out separately and sewn onto the body of the coat, so that the latter followed the figure more closely. Hips and chest were exaggerated by padding. Trousers either ended well above the ankles or were cut long enough to be strapped under the boots.

1825-1830

ALREADY, by 1827, the sleeves of gowns had begun to assume the swollen appearance so typical of the next decade. In ball dresses they looked like enormous epaulettes, which indeed was the name given to them. Skirts were growing wider, and the turned-down white collars larger, the Vandyke succeeding the Elizabethan. Hats were rounder and perched more on the top of the head. They were sometimes made of fine straw and worn over a small lace cap. Very long ribbons of the same colours as the trimming of the hat floated over the shoulders.

Chintzes came into favour for morning dresses, and for home costume during the day. Cambric skirts were bordered with shawl material, and a reticule of the same stuff was carried in the hand.

The corsage was longer in the waist than it had been, and the pleats of the skirt were gathered into the band, giving an equal fullness all round. This was known as the Dutch fashion, and did not last very long. Waists were very tight. Shawls of red cashmere were much worn as an outdoor covering.

1820-1830

TO the modern eye there is something very astonishing in the apparent unwillingness of women of the 'twenties ever to have their heads completely uncovered. The minimum for morning wear was an elaborate lace cap, and for evening, a towering wreath or some large ornament of metal. Very big hats with plumes were worn for dinner parties, and even at the opera—it is to be hoped, only by those who sat in boxes. Even so, a hat as broad as the lady's shoulders adorned with half-a-dozen immense ostrich feathers cannot have added much to the enjoyment of the attendant gallant.

Hair was sometimes parted on the forehead à la Madonna, with ringlets over each temple descending nearly as low as the tip of the ear. Sprigs of flowers were scattered among the bows in the hair, such bows being of coloured gauze ribbon striped with silver. Very high ornamental tortoiseshell combs were not unknown towards the end of the decade. They sustained two large curls, known as the Apollo's knot. Ball dresses were cut fairly low in a boat shape, and were very elaborately trimmed at the edge of the corsage.

1830

THE distinguishing feature of women's dress in the 'thirties was its enormous breadth caused by the width of the skirt and the extreme fullness of the sleeves. Skirts were short, and this exaggerated the squat impression of the whole costume. The sleeves were so voluminous, even in evening-dress, that they had to be kept extended by wicker frames or even by small feather cushions.

Hair-dressing was very elaborate, the hair being built up from the head and crowned with flowers, feathers, or jewelled combs. During the mourning for George IV, black and white crape flowers were used to decorate the hair in full dress.

Leghorn, rice straw, and *gros de Naples* were the materials most in favour for promenade hats, the brims of which were very wide, and cut so as to conceal as little of the face as possible. They were trimmed with dahlias, anemones, and field-flowers, sometimes mingled with ears of corn.

Full dress tended to be fairly simple, muslin being most usual; and, when mourning was over, this was generally white. If coloured, dresses were of one colour only, the favourites being rose, blue, or lilac.

1830-1835

IN the early 'thirties corsages were tight at the waist
and long, the heart-shaped bodice being the most
popular. Velvet was very much worn, even in combination
with silk. Crape, and a material called "blond," were also
used, and it was possible to have a dress *à la Taglioni* of tulle
worked in lamy. Printed satins were much in use for scarfs
and shawls. Poplin dresses were trimmed with satin bows.
Quite young women at balls or parties wore brocaded gauze
dresses of pink or white, or white organdie dresses, with a
rose in the hair and a rose at the girdle. Fashionable
colours of the early 'thirties were pink, blue, "grenat,"
violet de Parme, and lapis-lazuli; but yellow was a favourite
colour for ball dresses.

Shoes were flat-heeled and square-toed, and for evening
wear were generally of black satin. Silk stockings were very
fine and transparent, but it was the custom to wear another
pair underneath, of flesh-coloured cashmere.

The so-called Grecian coiffure was very fashionable, but
hair was also worn in plain bands or with ringlets wide apart
on the temples and descending low on the cheeks.

1835-1840

THE place of the fichu was taken by various kinds of collar, generally worn low and turned back. Collars could be made of plain velvet or of watered silk embroidered in colour. Tight sleeves or sleeves enlarging just above the elbow (known as sleeves *à la jardinière*) took the place of the exaggerated sleeves of the early part of the decade. Skirts became considerably longer, and, as their weight was becoming oppressive, Paris dressmakers, in 1839, introduced a modified form of hoop which could be added to or disengaged from the corset at pleasure. However, the *crino zephir* (or horsehair tissue under petticoats) was still worn.

Shawls were worn even in summer, when they were made of muslin, lace, or net. Plain cashmere shawls with deep fringes were also fashionable.

Children's dresses were mostly made of muslin or cambric with lace insertion.

There was considerable elaboration of such details of the toilette as handkerchiefs. These were sometimes embroidered in red, blue, or brown, with the name of the owner in Gothic characters, surmounted by her coat-of-arms. Black silk mittens were extremely common.

1830-1840

DURING the early 'thirties curls were much worn, and sometimes these were supported by wire frames and ornamental combs.

Towards the end of the decade the coiffure became very much lower, and many women, especially among the young, wore twists of hair falling on the neck, fastened with Italian pins. Long ringlets made their appearance, and sometimes the hair falling on the cheek was twisted spirally and the ends placed behind the ears.

The poke-bonnet was almost universal, but an attempt was made to raise it from the face by pulling down the brim at the sides. Then the crown was lowered, and at the end of the decade the whole hat was much smaller, although the peak was still fairly high. Straw hats became very general towards 1840. They were trimmed with crape or gauze of the same colour as the hat, or with field-flowers placed very far back on the brim. About 1839 an extraordinary substitute for the cap was introduced. This was the " arcade," which consisted of three or four wires in the form of a frame round which were twined rose-buds mixed with lace and ribbon.

1840

IF women have never dressed so scantily as they did about 1800, they have probably never been so warmly clad as in the 'forties. Five or six petticoats, with much solid padding, were quite normal, and worn as they were beneath long, full skirts, were of great advantage to the unshapely woman, as they concealed her natural deficiencies almost completely. But the weight of so many garments must have been intolerable, and the crinoline, when perfected, was a genuine reform. Shawls were still fashionable, and the poke bonnet had begun to assume its most characteristic shape.

Men's clothes had not yet abandoned all colour in deference to the growing fashion for black. The form of the frock-coat gave an almost feminine appearance to the male figure. Dress-coats also were extremely waisted. Tall hats were very high, and more shiny than they had been previously. Waistcoats were still elaborate and trousers very tight.

Riding became fashionable among both sexes, and the riding-habits of the period, with tight bodices (which were later slightly modified) and long, voluminous skirts, can be well studied in early paintings of Queen Victoria.

1840-1845

MANTELETS, or scarf-mantelets, became almost universal. They were made of tarlatan and tulle, and were worn over " chameleon " silk dresses. Silk mantelets were trimmed with ruches of lace, guipure, or shaded ribbon of a contrasting colour.

The laced corsage was sometimes adopted for the opportunity it offered of showing the chemisette, which was either embroidered or composed of insertions of lace. Ribbons were extensively used for the decoration of the upper part of the dress. Negligés are the natural result of tight lacing, although some of the so-called negligés of the 'forties would seem stiff enough to a generation accustomed to lounge in pyjamas. Men also had their lounging clothes or smoking suits, generally of a pseudo-Turkish appearance.

Hats were shorter at the ears and more forward in front than they had previously been. Sometimes they were composed of puffings of tulle ornamented with shaded feathers.

Ball dresses had several skirts and were usually ornamented with flowers.

1845-1850

CORSAGES continued to be tight, and were made either of plain silk or of puckered taffeta. " Volans," or flounces, almost superseded all other trimmings for dresses, sometimes as many as eight being adopted, the highest reaching to within a few inches of the waist. They could be made of fringe or of puckered lace. Skirts without " volans " sometimes had a kind of stylised apron. Dresses of light materials such as *barège*, silk, muslin, or coloured tarlatan had the sleeves puckered at the wristband. Large shawls of black or white lace, or of cashmere, alternated with mantelets or *visites*—a *visite* being a kind of three-quarter-length coat with sleeves made of embroidered muslin or some similar material. Towards the end of the decade, and for cold weather, a short coat called a " Casaweck " made its appearance, made of wadded satin or velvet. Alternatives were Castilian or Andalusian cloaks made of satin, or velvet Hungarian cloaks lined with ermine, minever, or chinchilla.

Small girls' dresses were mostly made with double skirts and with fan-shaped corsages cut straight on the chest and shoulders. The bonnet for out-of-doors was very similar to that worn by their elders.

1840-1850

ALTHOUGH ball dresses were very low, and neck and shoulders bare, there was a surprising absence of neck-jewellery, a simple brooch in the front of the corsage being considered sufficient. Indeed, an attempt seems to have been made, in making the neck and shoulders the only unadorned portion of an elaborate toilette, to draw particular attention to them, and it is certainly true that in the evening dresses of the period the appearance given to the female form of emerging from complicated wrappings could be used by a clever dressmaker with most seductive effect.

Hats were composed of tulle, straw, gauze, and flowers. Open straw hats were fashionable for warm weather, and about 1846 there was a return to the eighteenth-century mode, with a hat *à la Clarissa Harlowe*, much worn at watering-places or in the country.

The beginning of the decade witnessed a great variety of male neck-wear. Some cravats were worn, as well as neck-cloths tied in a bow in front. Cravats gradually disappeared, however, and narrow ties, over which the shirt collar could be folded, were adopted by the younger men. The " dicky," or separate shirt-front, was no longer worn, being replaced by a shirt with an inset breast of finer linen. Side-whiskers, worn with a moustache and small " Imperial," were not uncommon, although they had not yet attained the extravagant dimensions of a few years later.

1850

A GENERAL levelling of the classes took place, caused partly by the new passion for travel introduced by the extension of railways ; but the novel social conditions, if they tended to make rank less important, made wealth more so, and, therefore, gave added impetus to the competition of elegance.

The main features of women's dress may be briefly summarised. Skirts were very full and often heavily flounced. The corsage was sometimes open to the waist, so as to allow the white under-garment to be seen, the two edges of the corset being kept together by ribbons or narrow strips of cloth attached by buttons. Fairly wide sleeves ending half-way down the forearm, with a sleeve of softer material appearing beneath and gathered in at the wrist, are very typical of the period. When a series of false sleeves of different lengths were worn they were called Pagodas, and were frequently white. Small over-jackets or " cannezouts " of white embroidered muslin, bordered with English lace, were much seen about 1850. The poke-bonnet was smaller than before and the top line of the head almost horizontal. Very few changes are to be noted in male dress.

1850-1855

THE dominating influence in European fashion was, since her marriage in November 1853, the Empress Eugénie. Perhaps her Spanish taste had something to do with the growing rage for violent colour, but for evening wear she added her own influence to the prevailing fashion for white. The materials used were embroidered muslin and tulle, and the panniers of dresses were enriched with ribbons of white taffeta placed at the edge to give the effect of lace. Morning dresses were of thicker stuff, such as worsted poplin. With summer costumes mantillas were worn (another sign of Spanish influence), as well as shawls of muslin or white tarlatan. For winter there was great variety of cloaks, the colours of which were dark: red, brown, and drab. Velvet was used as a trimming for everything—hats, cloaks, and dresses. Sometimes velvet was embroidered with beads, particularly coral, and sometimes it was cut to represent pansies or daisies.

Hats were of Italian straw with flowers within and without, and were furnished with a single broad ribbon of taffeta tied beneath the chin in a simple bow. Sometimes they were made of velvet and crape combined, or of velvet and silk, or of velvet and lace. Velvet, always velvet!

1855-1860

FASHION in the late 'fifties was singularly stable, and the only " decided novelty " which a contemporary record can discover is a slight increase in the size of bonnets. It was felt that the diminutive bonnet, hanging on the back of the head, was out of proportion to the mass of silk lace and other trimmings comprising a fashionable dress. An attempt was made to break the rigidity of the triangle into which woman had reduced her figure, although the method adopted—an enlargement of sleeves—had the effect of concealing the narrowness of the waist, and so intensifying the triangular effect.

Skirts were heavily flounced, and the favourite materials for ball dresses were tulle, crape, or tarlatan. Pearls, and other gems, were fashionable as trimming, being used to gather in festoons the flounces of the dress. The sleeves of a bodice of 1857 are described as terminating in bracelets of coral.

Sleeves, which were considered as articles of lingerie, were extremely elaborate, sometimes consisting of puffed muslin or tulle confined at the wrist with coloured ribbon, and enriched with five or six rows of Valenciennes lace.

Boys' dresses were more sensibly designed than formerly, but little girls were still burdened with a mass of frills and feathers borrowed from the fashions of their elders.

1850-1860

THE Paris Exhibition of 1855, which was visited in state by Queen Victoria, had the effect of confirming the dominance of French fashions and facilitating their entry into England, and in nothing was the influence of France more potent than in millinery fashions. Bonnets, which tended to be placed very far back on the head, showing the hair as far back as the crown, were small but elaborate, artificial flowers (usually roses) being the most usual decoration. For indoor wear white muslin caps were popular, worked with ribbon or embroidery, and for the country or for sunny days some curiously wide hats were designed, made of rice straw, with a deep tulle fringe depending from the brim all the way round.

For the dressing of the hair, as for the trimming of the rest of the costume, there was, particularly towards the end of the decade, a rage for pearls. Hair-nets to enclose what was called the "torsade" of hair at the back of the head, were composed of strings of pearls, and these nets were edged with pearl fringe, with tassels of pearl at the back and sides and a "cordon" of pearls passed between the bandeaux of hair in front. Two or three rows of gold chain were sometimes worn in the same fashion. Ribbon head-dresses of pink, blue, cerise, or the popular *bouton d'or* were worn at the theatre.

With evening-dress carved and inlaid fans of mother-of-pearl or ivory were fashionable. They could also be made of black or white crape, spangled with gold or silver ornaments in the Spanish style.

1860

IT was in the early 'sixties that the crinoline achieved its most astonishing proportions. Woman's form was reduced to an isosceles triangle, for even the narrowness of the waist was concealed by the width of sleeves or the amplitude of cloaks. The effect was completed by the smallness of the head-wear, with the hair confined in close-fitting bonnets tied with a bow under the chin. A pretty face was all that was needed to be irresistible, for every other portion of the female figure was most effectively concealed. In France, the hey-day of the Second Empire was a period of great luxury and ostentation. Ball dresses, especially, were costly and magnificent, and precious stones began to be worn in ever-increasing numbers. In England the influence of the Court was calculated to restrain rather than to encourage extravagance, and the death of the Prince Consort in 1861 threw a cloud over social functions, which lasted for many years. However, the reign of the crinoline was just as lasting in England as in France, and even the dresses of little girls revealed the influence of the prevailing fashion. Men's formal attire showed very little change.

1860-1865

THE " pork-pie " hat and the chignon are very characteristic of the early years of the decade.

The crinoline was sometimes worn in the street with a skirt raised several inches from the ground, revealing ankle-boots or miniature Hessians, a fashion much caricatured and exaggerated in the pages of *Punch*. The drawing-up process (if the skirts were not cut short) was effected by a machine called the *cage américain*, an improvement on the ordinary crinoline.

For men, the sack coat and hard round hat made their appearance at much the same time as the famous " Dundreary " whiskers. Nothing is perhaps so strange to the modern eye as the latter, and their universality makes the period seem more foreign than much more distant epochs. Male attire became even more sombre than before, for the fancy waistcoat disappeared, and was succeeded by one made of the same material as the coat. Trousers, however, remained strongly patterned.

Dresses, for out-of-doors, were in general simple in cut and dark in colour, but when they were drawn up by interior laces, they revealed brightly coloured underskirts. For evening dresses light velvets in such colours as rose, pale green, lilac, or turquoise were much admired. Light cloth coats could be worn over dark dresses, and the Empress Eugénie started a fashion for various shades of brown *foulard des Indes* trimmed with black velvet.

1865-1870

THERE was a pronounced change in the shape of the skirt about 1868. It ceased to be triangular, to become more bottle-shaped, and by the end of the decade was only full behind. It is possible that the origin of the bustle is to be sought in the practice of looping up the outer skirt. By 1868 the underskirt had, in some dresses, become the important one, the upper skirt being caught up almost to the hips by interior fastenings. These fastenings were usually higher at the side than at the back, and the general effect is not very different from that of the typical dress of the early 'seventies. The supposition is strengthened by the appearance of dresses in which the overskirt was not drawn up. The back of the skirt descends in a straight, sloping line from the waist to the ground. There is no trace of the protuberance which was afterwards to become so exaggerated.

Underskirts and overskirts were sometimes worn in contrasting colours, but more frequently in different shades of the same colour. Combinations of brown silk and bright blue taffeta, or of green, and green and black checked taffeta, were not uncommon. Taffeta, indeed, seemed to have replaced velvet as the most popular material.

1860-1870

IN the early 'sixties women's hair assumed the typical chignon form, with the back hair confined in a net bag which hung from the top of the head to below the nape of the neck. Even when no net was used the form of hair-dressing was very much the same, and what modifications were attempted were to be seen chiefly in evening toilettes.

In the late 'sixties the hair was dressed very flat on top, with a large bun, sometimes almost the size of the head, projecting straight back. Sometimes it was worn loose over the shoulders with very youthful effect, or else with two long curls hanging down behind, almost to the waist. The hat continued to be the smallest part of the head-dress, completely failing to cover what was still called the chignon, although its characteristic form had been abandoned. Sometimes the hair was dressed in a cascade of curls at the back of the head, echoing very closely in its complicated convolutions the shape of the back of the skirt with its incipient bustle.

Men were in general bearded, and if they shaved at all it was generally the upper lip that was left bare. Hair was worn much longer than would be thought correct to-day, and was frequently brushed forward to produce curls above the ears.

1870

THE crinoline, as we have seen, disappeared in the late
'sixties, and women's dresses assumed the bunched-
up-behind appearance which they retained (with some
important modifications) for twenty years. But it was not
only the shape of dresses which was modified. The effect
of the War of 1870–71 on France, and hence on the whole
world of Fashion, was considerable. The luxury and
ostentation of the Empire were felt to be out of place, and
greater simplicity prevailed both in material and in ornamentation. The new mood did not last long, and accessories
of the *toilette* assumed a new importance, in particular gloves,
which were better made and more carefully chosen than they
had ever been before. The discovery of Japanese art served
to revive the interest in fans.

In men's dress a new informality was creeping in, marked
by the growing success of the sack coat, the ancestor of our
modern lounge suit. From having been something of an
eccentricity it became very common, and but for the fact
that trousers were of a different material from the coat and
waistcoat, the male dress of about 1870 would seem more
modern than many of the fashions that were to follow it.

1870-1875

THE corsage usually had the effect of a cavalryman's tunic, the skirts of the jacket projecting over the bustle. The draped appearance of the back of the skirt was universal, and skirts had a great many narrow flounces. Walking dresses touched the ground and some were even provided with a train. The cut of the dresses became very complicated, and a contemporary writer complains that whereas in former times an outmoded dress could still be used for something, in the 'seventies garments were composed of so many fragments of different materials that their only after-use was for the manufacture of patch-work quilts. It was the general custom to cut the dress out of two different materials, one patterned, one plain, and then to make one portion of the dress of the plain material trimmed with the patterned, and the rest of the patterned material trimmed with the plain. Check patterns were in great demand, and colours sometimes strident.

In the early 'seventies the mass of curls at the back of the head assumed, sometimes, monstrous proportions. The hair was also dressed higher at the back than it had been, with the result that the hat, which was still small, was pushed forward over the forehead.

1875-1880

ALREADY, by 1876, the bustle was much less pronounced, and that smoothness over the hips so characteristic of the early 'eighties had begun to make its appearance. Trimmings were elaborate, lace itself being used, not as formerly only at the edges of garments, but sewn onto their surface in *cascades, chutes,* or *ondulations.* There were shawls, fichus, and scarves in plenty, although a fashion writer of the period remarks that they were likely to be draped anywhere rather than round the neck.

Dresses tended to be comparatively simple in front and extremely complicated behind, with back fastenings (genuine or for ornament) of knots, bows, and even of fringed tassels.

A favourite material was " faye," either for evening or morning dresses, as it could be worked with embroidery or combined with figured velvet. Favourite colours were verdigris, blue marine, or pale blue, but the corsage was sometimes constructed, in deliberate contrast, of some such material as garnet velvet. Indian shawls were much used, worked up into the fashionable shapes of dolman or polonaise.

1870-1880

HATS, throughout the decade, tended to be very small, and perched high on the head. They were frequently made of felt, with extremely narrow brims and high crowns. To lift the hat still farther from the head the trimming was frequently placed underneath the front brim as well as on top. Little feather toques were worn for variety, as well as hats made entirely of ribbon. The bonnet had become so reduced in size as to be distinguished from the hat, if at all, only by the ribbon tied beneath the wearer's chin.

There is usually a consonance between the general form of dress and the form of coiffure. Hair, like clothes, tended to be drawn backwards, leaving the front of the head-dress comparatively simple and falling downwards at the back in a complicated arrangement of bands and twists reminiscent of the folds and flounces at the back of the skirt. This effect was enhanced by the fashion of weaving into the hair strands of ribbon or sprays of foliage. The face was left very free, and the ears were almost always visible.

1880

THE bustle may now be said to have disappeared, although
it was to appear again later.   However, although the
bustle had gone, dresses were still looped up behind, but
lower.   The back of the dress still tended to be its most
elaborate part.   The figure was treated as a framework on
which fringed draperies could be looped and crossed, much
in the fashion of the heavy window curtains of the period.
Waists were very narrow, and they accentuated the apparent
rigidity of the form beneath its wrappings.   An attempt was
made to keep the top portion of the costume very sleek,
following as closely as possible the lines of the corset, and
then below the hips to flare out in frills, and bows, and
trimmings.

Colours were violent, plum trimmed with electric blue,
or royal blue with an edging of scarlet being not uncommon.
Their garishness was, however, mitigated by the almost
invariable custom of wearing white lace frills at the throat
and wrists.   Evening-gowns were, in general, not cut so
low as they had been.   Men's dress had assumed its modern
hue and cut.

1880-1885

THE eclipse of the bustle was very brief. Indeed, it appeared in an exaggerated form fairly early in the new decade. There was a revival of interest in the Empire period, although so-called Empire dresses bore only the most shadowy resemblance to their prototypes. The simplicity of the Empire style was entirely lacking. Extremely complicated dresses were constructed of taffeta and tulle combined, three skirts of the latter being frequently superimposed on a " sheath-skirt " of the former, or a skirt of silk was decorated with three, five, or seven "volans" of pleated tulle.

Day gowns had a certain " tailor-made " effect, especially in the bodice, which lent itself to the use of somewhat heavy materials, of which wool was the chief constituent. Hats were, in general, small, and somewhat masculine in shape, and their decoration—feathers, ribbons, or artificial flowers—was discreet. The very small bonnet tied with broad ribbons under the chin was still fashionable. The hair was worn fairly close to the head.

1885-1890

DRESSES, in the second half of the decade, were somewhat shorter, although the bustle was as pronounced
as it had ever been. Bodices were not quite so masculine in
cut. They followed the lines of the figure very closely, but
the hard line between bodice and skirt was, in general, less
noticeable. The liking for woollen materials persisted, and
there was a rage of Scottish plaid patterns even in Paris.
For evening toilettes for very young women it was usual
to have a corsage of satin and a skirt of gauze, generally of
different colours. Those who did not desire to dance wore
trains. *Décolletage* was not extreme. After being eclipsed
for a time by the *décolleté en cœur*, the square opening came
back into favour, although for those who were afraid of
being thought too thin the round opening was preferred.
White gloves were, of course, *de rigeur*, and precious stones,
particularly diamonds, were worn in great numbers. Hats
were still sometimes worn at the theatre, but were so small
as to cause little inconvenience. Hats for the street were also
extremely small, although the trimming was sometimes built
up to a considerable height. Hair was dressed in a small
bun on the very top of the head.

The straw hat for men became very popular, not only for
boating, but the silk hat held its own for ordinary wear.

1880-1890

WOMEN'S hats in this decade were, in general, small, and hair-dressing comparatively simple. A kind of compromise was evolved between the hat and the bonnet with strings, and the result grew less and less like the latter, and more and more like the former. Plumes, artificial flowers, and a blend of the two became fashionable, and complete stuffed birds were sometimes used for the trimming of hats. The hat tended to rise more and more off the head as the decade progressed, and in 1890 the front brim, which was much larger than the rest of the hat, rose steeply above the forehead. The male straw hat and felt hat were adopted by women with sporting inclinations.

Men's headgear showed a new informality. The bowler hat and the fishing cap (with brim all round) made their appearance. Vests were buttoned very high, and very little linen was exposed to view. Whiskers were no longer worn, but the moustache was almost universal.

1890

IN England, costume is inevitably modified, from time to time, in the direction of informality, by the influence of country life.   The male fashions of the early nineteenth century all over Europe were the direct outcome of the Englishman's passion for riding.   These fashions had gradually been formalised, and the new enthusiasm for athletics at the end of the century led to the invention of the " Norfolk jacket " and the re-discovery of knickerbockers.   The complete monopoly of trousers, which had lasted since the early years of the century, was over at last.

Women's walking dresses were still cumbrous enough, and still too tight-waisted, but even in feminine attire the influence of sport was beginning to make itself felt.   About 1890 also began the passion for fine underclothes, which has lasted until our own day, and was perhaps originally provoked by the plainness of the fashionable tailor-made. It seemed an added refinement to allow luxuries of dress to be almost, if not entirely, concealed beneath a plain exterior.   The manufacture of extremely fine materials received an immense impetus from the new demand.

1890-1895

ONE of the distinguishing marks of the early 'nineties was the revival of the wide sleeves of 1830. Indeed, Fashion has probably never so nearly repeated itself. The silhouette of 1830 and that of 1895 are almost identical, except that in the former the skirt was considerably shorter and the waist not so narrow. Some of the hats were surprisingly similar also, although the method of hair-dressing was different. The main difference in the sleeve was that in the 'nineties only the upper arm was puffed, giving rise to the famous " leg-of-mutton " appearance so typical of the period.

Skirts were long and trailing, but were comparatively simple in cut. The " wasp-waist " had assumed its most exaggerated and pernicious form. The bodice was close-fitting, and so great was the importance attached to sleeves that even in evening-dress small puffs of ribbon were sometimes attached to the shoulders to give the fashionable effect. In the street, muffs were almost universally carried, and were small, so that they could be carried on one forearm, the other hand being perpetually occupied in lifting the dress.

1895-1900

EVENING dresses, so long as the puffed sleeve was given its due importance, could be cut very low in front, but in general bodices were designed to fit closely round the neck, and occasionally a miniature Elizabethan ruffle was added behind. A considerable quantity of often costly lace was worn, at the wrists or in the form of a frilled shirt front attached to the corsage.

Capes were fashionable throughout the decade, and their forms, echoing those of the garments, were sometimes provided with raised shoulders.

The " Norfolk jacket " for men has been already mentioned. Cycling brought in knickerbockers for women, worn with over-tunics of mannish cut, and a very small hat. Children's dresses were more sensible than they had been for some time.

The most striking innovation during the last few years of the century was the blouse—thought to have been derived from the earlier " garibaldi," a shirt-like garment which, at first, was always red, like that of the Italian general from whom it took its name. The waist was still terribly constricted, but the wasp-like effect was diminished by allowing the bodice to hang over the now universal belt.

1890-1900

BLOUSES were popular, and their fronts could be very elaborate with heavy frills of Valenciennes lace. Necks were high, and in evening-dress were sometimes encircled somewhat tightly by four or five rows of pearls or brilliants, a fashion now associated in most minds with Queen Alexandra.

About 1895 the most fashionable hat was a very small toque, to which Bird of Paradise plumes, arranged in a vertical aigrette in the centre, were an almost inevitable addition. Jet was much prized as a decoration for millinery, and it could be mingled with artificial flowers of much exaggerated size—mammoth violets or gigantic roses. Spotted veils were common, especially with the very small hats. Towards the end of the decade there was a growing tendency for hats to have wider brims and to be placed flat on the top of the head.

Men often wore a single collar, straight up all the way round, with (in evening-dress) a rather small and very flat white tie. Moustaches were still worn by almost every man, but beards had largely gone out of favour.

1900

THE end of the century is reached, but there is as yet no sign of the revolution which is to take place in women's clothes during the next twenty-five years. The corset was designed to throw the hips back and the bust forward in the most exaggerated manner possible. The lines of clothes followed those of the so-called *Art Nouveau*, with its swirling curves and its restless decorations. Even walking dresses had long trains collecting the dust of the streets at every step. The influence of sport had already produced costumes of varying degrees of usefulness, but that influence had not yet begun to affect fashionable attire.

For men of almost every position formal dress was still the usual costume, and the silk hat still reigned supreme. Indeed, the century as a whole exhibits far less striking modifications of costume than might have been expected from what was, in every respect, so revolutionary an epoch. Yet the clothes of the Nineteenth Century, viewed in retrospect, seem curiously appropriate. There is an intimate connection between costumes and manners, but no one knows exactly what it is.

A CATALOG OF SELECTED DOVER
BOOKS IN ALL FIELDS OF INTEREST

CONCERNING THE SPIRITUAL IN ART, Wassily Kandinsky. Pioneering work by father of abstract art. Thoughts on color theory, nature of art. Analysis of earlier masters. 12 illustrations. 80pp. of text. 5⅜ x 8½. 23411-8 Pa. $4.95

ANIMALS: 1,419 Copyright-Free Illustrations of Mammals, Birds, Fish, Insects, etc., Jim Harter (ed.). Clear wood engravings present, in extremely lifelike poses, over 1,000 species of animals. One of the most extensive pictorial sourcebooks of its kind. Captions. Index. 284pp. 9 x 12. 23766-4 Pa. $14.95

CELTIC ART: The Methods of Construction, George Bain. Simple geometric techniques for making Celtic interlacements, spirals, Kells-type initials, animals, humans, etc. Over 500 illustrations. 160pp. 9 x 12. (USO) 22923-8 Pa. $9.95

AN ATLAS OF ANATOMY FOR ARTISTS, Fritz Schider. Most thorough reference work on art anatomy in the world. Hundreds of illustrations, including selections from works by Vesalius, Leonardo, Goya, Ingres, Michelangelo, others. 593 illustrations. 192pp. 7⅛ x 10¼. 20241-0 Pa. $9.95

CELTIC HAND STROKE-BY-STROKE (Irish Half-Uncial from "The Book of Kells"): An Arthur Baker Calligraphy Manual, Arthur Baker. Complete guide to creating each letter of the alphabet in distinctive Celtic manner. Covers hand position, strokes, pens, inks, paper, more. Illustrated. 48pp. 8¼ x 11. 24336-2 Pa. $3.95

EASY ORIGAMI, John Montroll. Charming collection of 32 projects (hat, cup, pelican, piano, swan, many more) specially designed for the novice origami hobbyist. Clearly illustrated easy-to-follow instructions insure that even beginning papercrafters will achieve successful results. 48pp. 8¼ x 11. 27298-2 Pa. $3.50

THE COMPLETE BOOK OF BIRDHOUSE CONSTRUCTION FOR WOODWORKERS, Scott D. Campbell. Detailed instructions, illustrations, tables. Also data on bird habitat and instinct patterns. Bibliography. 3 tables. 63 illustrations in 15 figures. 48pp. 5¼ x 8½. 24407-5 Pa. $2.50

BLOOMINGDALE'S ILLUSTRATED 1886 CATALOG: Fashions, Dry Goods and Housewares, Bloomingdale Brothers. Famed merchants' extremely rare catalog depicting about 1,700 products: clothing, housewares, firearms, dry goods, jewelry, more. Invaluable for dating, identifying vintage items. Also, copyright-free graphics for artists, designers. Co-published with Henry Ford Museum & Greenfield Village. 160pp. 8¼ x 11. 25780-0 Pa. $10.95

HISTORIC COSTUME IN PICTURES, Braun & Schneider. Over 1,450 costumed figures in clearly detailed engravings—from dawn of civilization to end of 19th century. Captions. Many folk costumes. 256pp. 8⅜ x 11¾. 23150-X Pa. $12.95

STICKLEY CRAFTSMAN FURNITURE CATALOGS, Gustav Stickley and L. & J. G. Stickley. Beautiful, functional furniture in two authentic catalogs from 1910. 594 illustrations, including 277 photos, show settles, rockers, armchairs, reclining chairs, bookcases, desks, tables. 183pp. 6½ x 9¼. 23838-5 Pa. $11.95

AMERICAN LOCOMOTIVES IN HISTORIC PHOTOGRAPHS: 1858 to 1949, Ron Ziel (ed.). A rare collection of 126 meticulously detailed official photographs, called "builder portraits," of American locomotives that majestically chronicle the rise of steam locomotive power in America. Introduction. Detailed captions. xi + 129pp. 9 x 12. 27393-8 Pa. $13.95

AMERICA'S LIGHTHOUSES: An Illustrated History, Francis Ross Holland, Jr. Delightfully written, profusely illustrated fact-filled survey of over 200 American lighthouses since 1716. History, anecdotes, technological advances, more. 240pp. 8 x 10¾. 25576-X Pa. $12.95

TOWARDS A NEW ARCHITECTURE, Le Corbusier. Pioneering manifesto by founder of "International School." Technical and aesthetic theories, views of industry, economics, relation of form to function, "mass-production split" and much more. Profusely illustrated. 320pp. 6⅛ x 9¼. (USO) 25023-7 Pa. $9.95

HOW THE OTHER HALF LIVES, Jacob Riis. Famous journalistic record, exposing poverty and degradation of New York slums around 1900, by major social reformer. 100 striking and influential photographs. 233pp. 10 x 7⅞. 22012-5 Pa. $11.95

FRUIT KEY AND TWIG KEY TO TREES AND SHRUBS, William M. Harlow. One of the handiest and most widely used identification aids. Fruit key covers 120 deciduous and evergreen species; twig key 160 deciduous species. Easily used. Over 300 photographs. 126pp. 5⅜ x 8½. 20511-8 Pa. $3.95

COMMON BIRD SONGS, Dr. Donald J. Borror. Songs of 60 most common U.S. birds: robins, sparrows, cardinals, bluejays, finches, more—arranged in order of increasing complexity. Up to 9 variations of songs of each species. Cassette and manual 99911-4 $8.95

ORCHIDS AS HOUSE PLANTS, Rebecca Tyson Northen. Grow cattleyas and many other kinds of orchids—in a window, in a case, or under artificial light. 63 illustrations. 148pp. 5⅜ x 8½. 23261-1 Pa. $5.95

MONSTER MAZES, Dave Phillips. Masterful mazes at four levels of difficulty. Avoid deadly perils and evil creatures to find magical treasures. Solutions for all 32 exciting illustrated puzzles. 48pp. 8¼ x 11. 26005-4 Pa. $2.95

MOZART'S DON GIOVANNI (DOVER OPERA LIBRETTO SERIES), Wolfgang Amadeus Mozart. Introduced and translated by Ellen H. Bleiler. Standard Italian libretto, with complete English translation. Convenient and thoroughly portable—an ideal companion for reading along with a recording or the performance itself. Introduction. List of characters. Plot summary. 121pp. 5¼ x 8½. 24944-1 Pa. $3.95

TECHNICAL MANUAL AND DICTIONARY OF CLASSICAL BALLET, Gail Grant. Defines, explains, comments on steps, movements, poses and concepts. 15-page pictorial section. Basic book for student, viewer. 127pp. 5⅜ x 8½. 21843-0 Pa. $4.95

BRASS INSTRUMENTS: Their History and Development, Anthony Baines. Authoritative, updated survey of the evolution of trumpets, trombones, bugles, cornets, French horns, tubas and other brass wind instruments. Over 140 illustrations and 48 music examples. Corrected and updated by author. New preface. Bibliography. 320pp. 5⅜ x 8½. 27574-4 Pa. $9.95

HOLLYWOOD GLAMOR PORTRAITS, John Kobal (ed.). 145 photos from 1926-49. Harlow, Gable, Bogart, Bacall; 94 stars in all. Full background on photographers, technical aspects. 160pp. 8⅜ x 11¼. 23352-9 Pa. $12.95

MAX AND MORITZ, Wilhelm Busch. Great humor classic in both German and English. Also 10 other works: "Cat and Mouse," "Plisch and Plumm," etc. 216pp. 5⅜ x 8½. 20181-3 Pa. $6.95

THE RAVEN AND OTHER FAVORITE POEMS, Edgar Allan Poe. Over 40 of the author's most memorable poems: "The Bells," "Ulalume," "Israfel," "To Helen," "The Conqueror Worm," "Eldorado," "Annabel Lee," many more. Alphabetic lists of titles and first lines. 64pp. 5$\frac{3}{16}$ x 8¼. 26685-0 Pa. $1.00

PERSONAL MEMOIRS OF U. S. GRANT, Ulysses Simpson Grant. Intelligent, deeply moving firsthand account of Civil War campaigns, considered by many the finest military memoirs ever written. Includes letters, historic photographs, maps and more. 528pp. 6⅛ x 9¼. 28587-1 Pa. $12.95

AMULETS AND SUPERSTITIONS, E. A. Wallis Budge. Comprehensive discourse on origin, powers of amulets in many ancient cultures: Arab, Persian Babylonian, Assyrian, Egyptian, Gnostic, Hebrew, Phoenician, Syriac, etc. Covers cross, swastika, crucifix, seals, rings, stones, etc. 584pp. 5⅜ x 8½. 23573-4 Pa. $15.95

RUSSIAN STORIES/PYCCKNE PACCKA3bl: A Dual-Language Book, edited by Gleb Struve. Twelve tales by such masters as Chekhov, Tolstoy, Dostoevsky, Pushkin, others. Excellent word-for-word English translations on facing pages, plus teaching and study aids, Russian/English vocabulary, biographical/critical introductions, more. 416pp. 5⅜ x 8½. 26244-8 Pa. $9.95

PHILADELPHIA THEN AND NOW: 60 Sites Photographed in the Past and Present, Kenneth Finkel and Susan Oyama. Rare photographs of City Hall, Logan Square, Independence Hall, Betsy Ross House, other landmarks juxtaposed with contemporary views. Captures changing face of historic city. Introduction. Captions. 128pp. 8¼ x 11. 25790-8 Pa. $9.95

AIA ARCHITECTURAL GUIDE TO NASSAU AND SUFFOLK COUNTIES, LONG ISLAND, The American Institute of Architects, Long Island Chapter, and the Society for the Preservation of Long Island Antiquities. Comprehensive, well-researched and generously illustrated volume brings to life over three centuries of Long Island's great architectural heritage. More than 240 photographs with authoritative, extensively detailed captions. 176pp. 8¼ x 11. 26946-9 Pa. $14.95

NORTH AMERICAN INDIAN LIFE: Customs and Traditions of 23 Tribes, Elsie Clews Parsons (ed.). 27 fictionalized essays by noted anthropologists examine religion, customs, government, additional facets of life among the Winnebago, Crow, Zuni, Eskimo, other tribes. 480pp. 6⅛ x 9¼. 27377-6 Pa. $10.95

FRANK LLOYD WRIGHT'S HOLLYHOCK HOUSE, Donald Hoffmann. Lavishly illustrated, carefully documented study of one of Wright's most controversial residential designs. Over 120 photographs, floor plans, elevations, etc. Detailed perceptive text by noted Wright scholar. Index. 128pp. 9¼ x 10¾. 27133-1 Pa. $11.95

THE MALE AND FEMALE FIGURE IN MOTION: 60 Classic Photographic Sequences, Eadweard Muybridge. 60 true-action photographs of men and women walking, running, climbing, bending, turning, etc., reproduced from rare 19th-century masterpiece. vi + 121pp. 9 x 12. 24745-7 Pa. $10.95

1001 QUESTIONS ANSWERED ABOUT THE SEASHORE, N. J. Berrill and Jacquelyn Berrill. Queries answered about dolphins, sea snails, sponges, starfish, fishes, shore birds, many others. Covers appearance, breeding, growth, feeding, much more. 305pp. 5¼ x 8¼. 23366-9 Pa. $9.95

GUIDE TO OWL WATCHING IN NORTH AMERICA, Donald S. Heintzelman. Superb guide offers complete data and descriptions of 19 species: barn owl, screech owl, snowy owl, many more. Expert coverage of owl-watching equipment, conservation, migrations and invasions, etc. Guide to observing sites. 84 illustrations. xiii + 193pp. 5⅜ x 8½. 27344-X Pa. $8.95

MEDICINAL AND OTHER USES OF NORTH AMERICAN PLANTS: A Historical Survey with Special Reference to the Eastern Indian Tribes, Charlotte Erichsen-Brown. Chronological historical citations document 500 years of usage of plants, trees, shrubs native to eastern Canada, northeastern U.S. Also complete identifying information. 343 illustrations. 544pp. 6½ x 9¼. 25951-X Pa. $12.95

STORYBOOK MAZES, Dave Phillips. 23 stories and mazes on two-page spreads: Wizard of Oz, Treasure Island, Robin Hood, etc. Solutions. 64pp. 8¼ x 11. 23628-5 Pa. $2.95

NEGRO FOLK MUSIC, U.S.A., Harold Courlander. Noted folklorist's scholarly yet readable analysis of rich and varied musical tradition. Includes authentic versions of over 40 folk songs. Valuable bibliography and discography. xi + 324pp. 5⅜ x 8½. 27350-4 Pa. $9.95

MOVIE-STAR PORTRAITS OF THE FORTIES, John Kobal (ed.). 163 glamor, studio photos of 106 stars of the 1940s: Rita Hayworth, Ava Gardner, Marlon Brando, Clark Gable, many more. 176pp. 8⅜ x 11¼. 23546-7 Pa. $14.95

BENCHLEY LOST AND FOUND, Robert Benchley. Finest humor from early 30s, about pet peeves, child psychologists, post office and others. Mostly unavailable elsewhere. 73 illustrations by Peter Arno and others. 183pp. 5⅜ x 8½. 22410-4 Pa. $6.95

YEKL and THE IMPORTED BRIDEGROOM AND OTHER STORIES OF YIDDISH NEW YORK, Abraham Cahan. Film Hester Street based on Yekl (1896). Novel, other stories among first about Jewish immigrants on N.Y.'s East Side. 240pp. 5⅜ x 8½. 22427-9 Pa. $6.95

SELECTED POEMS, Walt Whitman. Generous sampling from *Leaves of Grass*. Twenty-four poems include "I Hear America Singing," "Song of the Open Road," "I Sing the Body Electric," "When Lilacs Last in the Dooryard Bloom'd," "O Captain! My Captain!"–all reprinted from an authoritative edition. Lists of titles and first lines. 128pp. 5³⁄₁₆ x 8¼. 26878-0 Pa. $1.00

THE BEST TALES OF HOFFMANN, E. T. A. Hoffmann. 10 of Hoffmann's most important stories: "Nutcracker and the King of Mice," "The Golden Flowerpot," etc. 458pp. 5⅜ x 8½. 21793-0 Pa. $9.95

FROM FETISH TO GOD IN ANCIENT EGYPT, E. A. Wallis Budge. Rich detailed survey of Egyptian conception of "God" and gods, magic, cult of animals, Osiris, more. Also, superb English translations of hymns and legends. 240 illustrations. 545pp. 5⅜ x 8½. 25803-3 Pa. $13.95

FRENCH STORIES/CONTES FRANÇAIS: A Dual-Language Book, Wallace Fowlie. Ten stories by French masters, Voltaire to Camus: "Micromegas" by Voltaire; "The Atheist's Mass" by Balzac; "Minuet" by de Maupassant; "The Guest" by Camus, six more. Excellent English translations on facing pages. Also French-English vocabulary list, exercises, more. 352pp. 5⅜ x 8½. 26443-2 Pa. $9.95

CHICAGO AT THE TURN OF THE CENTURY IN PHOTOGRAPHS: 122 Historic Views from the Collections of the Chicago Historical Society, Larry A. Viskochil. Rare large-format prints offer detailed views of City Hall, State Street, the Loop, Hull House, Union Station, many other landmarks, circa 1904-1913. Introduction. Captions. Maps. 144pp. 9⅜ x 12¼. 24656-6 Pa. $12.95

OLD BROOKLYN IN EARLY PHOTOGRAPHS, 1865-1929, William Lee Younger. Luna Park, Gravesend race track, construction of Grand Army Plaza, moving of Hotel Brighton, etc. 157 previously unpublished photographs. 165pp. 8⅞ x 11¾. 23587-4 Pa. $13.95

THE MYTHS OF THE NORTH AMERICAN INDIANS, Lewis Spence. Rich anthology of the myths and legends of the Algonquins, Iroquois, Pawnees and Sioux, prefaced by an extensive historical and ethnological commentary. 36 illustrations. 480pp. 5⅜ x 8½. 25967-6 Pa. $10.95

AN ENCYCLOPEDIA OF BATTLES: Accounts of Over 1,560 Battles from 1479 B.C. to the Present, David Eggenberger. Essential details of every major battle in recorded history from the first battle of Megiddo in 1479 B.C. to Grenada in 1984. List of Battle Maps. New Appendix covering the years 1967-1984. Index. 99 illustrations. 544pp. 6½ x 9¼. 24913-1 Pa. $16.95

SAILING ALONE AROUND THE WORLD, Captain Joshua Slocum. First man to sail around the world, alone, in small boat. One of great feats of seamanship told in delightful manner. 67 illustrations. 294pp. 5⅜ x 8½. 20326-3 Pa. $6.95

ANARCHISM AND OTHER ESSAYS, Emma Goldman. Powerful, penetrating, prophetic essays on direct action, role of minorities, prison reform, puritan hypocrisy, violence, etc. 271pp. 5⅜ x 8½. 22484-8 Pa. $7.95

MYTHS OF THE HINDUS AND BUDDHISTS, Ananda K. Coomaraswamy and Sister Nivedita. Great stories of the epics; deeds of Krishna, Shiva, taken from puranas, Vedas, folk tales; etc. 32 illustrations. 400pp. 5⅜ x 8½. 21759-0 Pa. $12.95

BEYOND PSYCHOLOGY, Otto Rank. Fear of death, desire of immortality, nature of sexuality, social organization, creativity, according to Rankian system. 291pp. 5⅜ x 8½. 20485-5 Pa. $8.95

A THEOLOGICO-POLITICAL TREATISE, Benedict Spinoza. Also contains unfinished Political Treatise. Great classic on religious liberty, theory of government on common consent. R. Elwes translation. Total of 421pp. 5⅜ x 8½. 20249-6 Pa. $9.95

CATALOG OF DOVER BOOKS

THE INFLUENCE OF SEA POWER UPON HISTORY, 1660–1783, A. T. Mahan. Influential classic of naval history and tactics still used as text in war colleges. First paperback edition. 4 maps. 24 battle plans. 640pp. 5⅜ x 8½.   25509-3 Pa. $14.95

THE STORY OF THE TITANIC AS TOLD BY ITS SURVIVORS, Jack Winocour (ed.). What it was really like. Panic, despair, shocking inefficiency, and a little heroism. More thrilling than any fictional account. 26 illustrations. 320pp. 5⅜ x 8½.
20610-6 Pa. $8.95

FAIRY AND FOLK TALES OF THE IRISH PEASANTRY, William Butler Yeats (ed.). Treasury of 64 tales from the twilight world of Celtic myth and legend: "The Soul Cages," "The Kildare Pooka," "King O'Toole and his Goose," many more. Introduction and Notes by W. B. Yeats. 352pp. 5⅜ x 8½.   26941-8 Pa. $8.95

BUDDHIST MAHAYANA TEXTS, E. B. Cowell and Others (eds.). Superb, accurate translations of basic documents in Mahayana Buddhism, highly important in history of religions. The Buddha-karita of Asvaghosha, Larger Sukhavativyuha, more. 448pp. 5⅜ x 8½.   25552-2 Pa. $12.95

ONE TWO THREE . . . INFINITY: Facts and Speculations of Science, George Gamow. Great physicist's fascinating, readable overview of contemporary science: number theory, relativity, fourth dimension, entropy, genes, atomic structure, much more. 128 illustrations. Index. 352pp. 5⅜ x 8½.   25664-2 Pa. $8.95

ENGINEERING IN HISTORY, Richard Shelton Kirby, et al. Broad, nontechnical survey of history's major technological advances: birth of Greek science, industrial revolution, electricity and applied science, 20th-century automation, much more. 181 illustrations. ". . . excellent . . ."–*Isis.* Bibliography. vii + 530pp. 5⅜ x 8¼.
26412-2 Pa. $14.95

DALÍ ON MODERN ART: The Cuckolds of Antiquated Modern Art, Salvador Dalí. Influential painter skewers modern art and its practitioners. Outrageous evaluations of Picasso, Cézanne, Turner, more. 15 renderings of paintings discussed. 44 calligraphic decorations by Dalí. 96pp. 5⅜ x 8½. (USO)   29220-7 Pa. $4.95

ANTIQUE PLAYING CARDS: A Pictorial History, Henry René D'Allemagne. Over 900 elaborate, decorative images from rare playing cards (14th–20th centuries): Bacchus, death, dancing dogs, hunting scenes, royal coats of arms, players cheating, much more. 96pp. 9¼ x 12¼.   29265-7 Pa. $12.95

MAKING FURNITURE MASTERPIECES: 30 Projects with Measured Drawings, Franklin H. Gottshall. Step-by-step instructions, illustrations for constructing handsome, useful pieces, among them a Sheraton desk, Chippendale chair, Spanish desk, Queen Anne table and a William and Mary dressing mirror. 224pp. 8⅛ x 11¼.
29338-6 Pa. $13.95

THE FOSSIL BOOK: A Record of Prehistoric Life, Patricia V. Rich et al. Profusely illustrated definitive guide covers everything from single-celled organisms and dinosaurs to birds and mammals and the interplay between climate and man. Over 1,500 illustrations. 760pp. 7½ x 10⅛.   29371-8 Pa. $29.95

Prices subject to change without notice.

Available at your book dealer or write for free catalog to Dept. GI, Dover Publications, Inc., 31 East 2nd St., Mineola, N.Y. 11501. Dover publishes more than 500 books each year on science, elementary and advanced mathematics, biology, music, art, literary history, social sciences and other areas.